THE HYGGE WITCHES ALMANAC

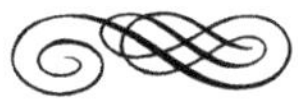

THE HYGGE WITCHES ALMANAC

CHARLOTTE MANN

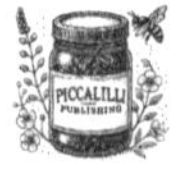

PICCALILLI PUBLISHING

Dedication...

For Pam, my mum, who showed me the beauty in simplicity and the joy found in life's small comforts. She taught me to cherish the glow of a campfire, the warmth of a soft blanket and the peace of a shared cup of tea. Through her, I learned that happiness isn't found in grand gestures, but rather in creating moments of cosiness, love and connection. Her wisdom and nurturing spirit made my world a softer, gentler place and because of that, I am endlessly blessed.

Always missed...

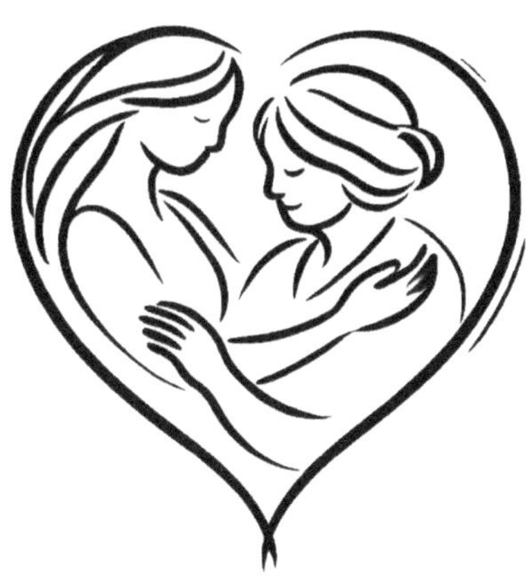

The Hygge Witch:

A person who blends the principles of their craft with the Danish concept of cosy and contented living.

These arts emphasise comfort, warmth and nurturing the spirit while honouring the cycles of nature and personal well - being. Hygge witches focus on creating a harmonious and welcoming environment which promotes relaxation, mindfulness and spiritual growth.

Their rituals often involve elements of warmth, fostered by, candles, warm drinks, crafts and comforting spaces. The intention is to integrate the magic of everyday life with practices that nurture contentment and joy.

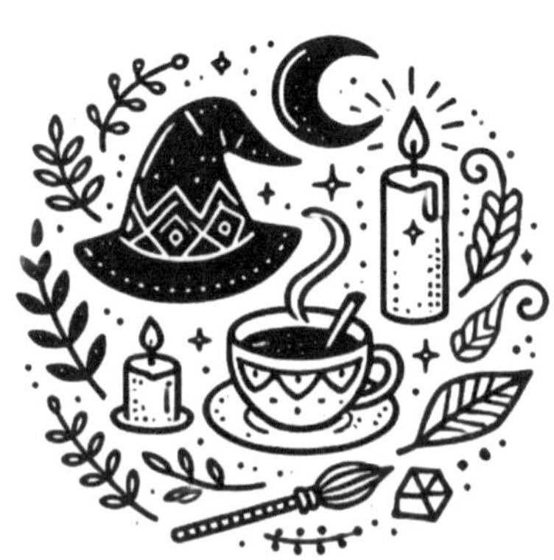

Embracing The Seasons With Connection.

This book is the first in a series of four - a heartfelt tribute to the rich and often misunderstood heritage of the witch.

It honours the resilience, wisdom and magick passed through the generations of healers, artists, oracles, doulas, visionaries, traders and martyrs. Celebrating the beauty of witchcraft in all its forms.

More than a rememberance of the past, it's a nod to the enduring spirit of the witch and a celebration of its place in the modern world.

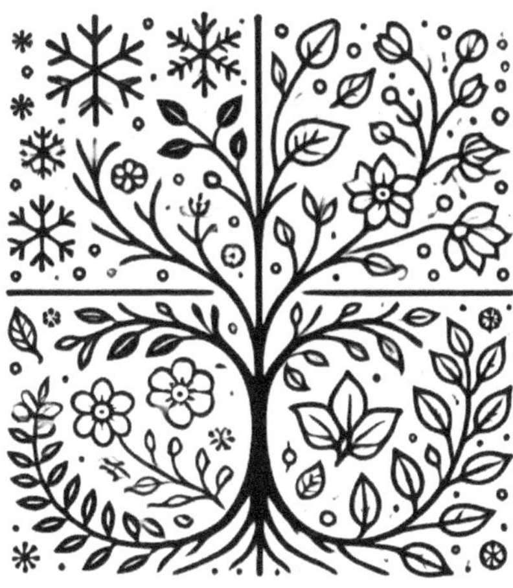

Contents

1

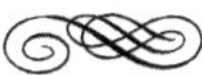

January

In January's chill, we gather sticks,
To build small fires with gentle clicks.
The smoke curls high, the flames glow bright,
Warming hands in the fading light.

Wooly jumpers pulled on tight,
Against the cold, we brace the night.
With frosty breath and skies of grey,
We face the heart of Winter's day.

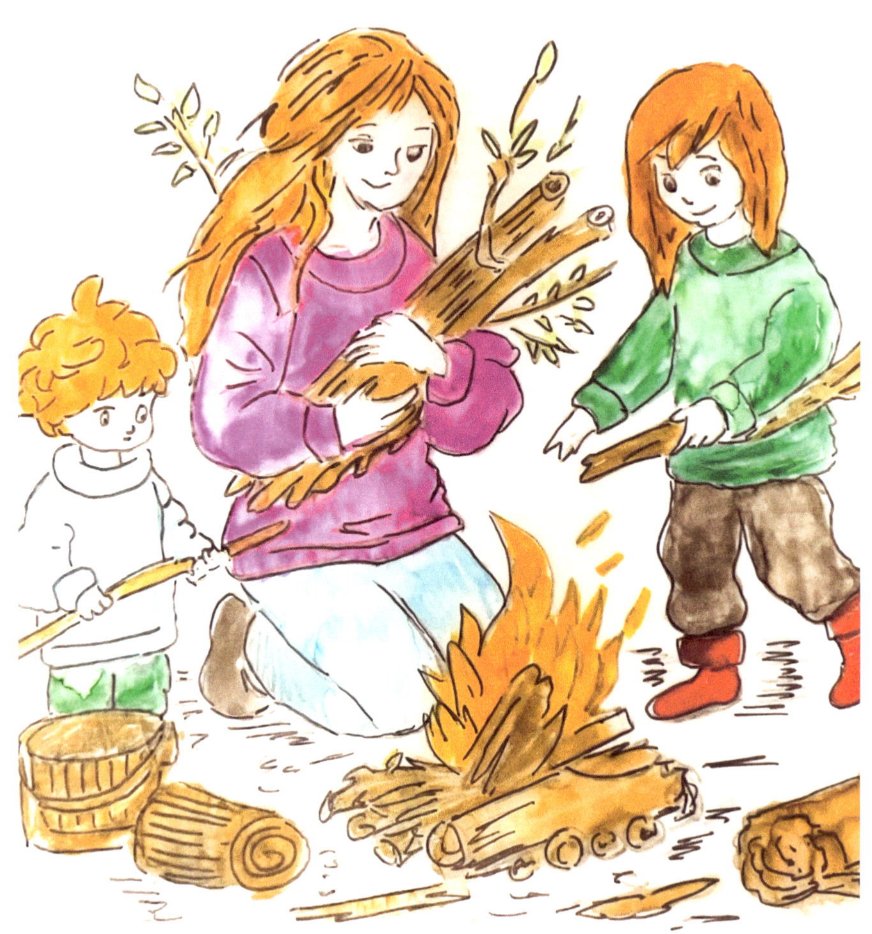

January is a time for stillness, resilience and preparation for the renewal that comes with Spring. It can be about honouring the dark, nurturing the seeds of new beginnings and maintaining a connection to nature and community. It is a good time to come together, even virtually and share knowledge and support during darker months. This is a time for storytelling, sharing wisdom alongside those with similar beliefs.

Given the dark and cold nature of January, it is a time for introspection and inner work. Many use meditative practices or journaling which could include working on resolutions for self-growth, healing old emotional wounds and setting intentions which align with natural cycles.

January rituals may involve herbs and scents such as cedar, juniper and sage, which are known for their cleansing and protective properties. Crystals, garnet and onyx are commonly used at this time for grounding and augmenting strength. Colours such as silver, white and dark green represent Winter's purity and endurance. Simple rituals involving lighting candles, chanting and using water and incense for purification can help us to feel connected and renewed.

January's stillness can be observed in the survival of wildlife during the harshest phase of Winter. Spending time in natural settings, leave offerings for animals and reflect on the resilience of nature. This practice strengthens the connection with Earth and acknowledges the subtle changes that lead to Spring.

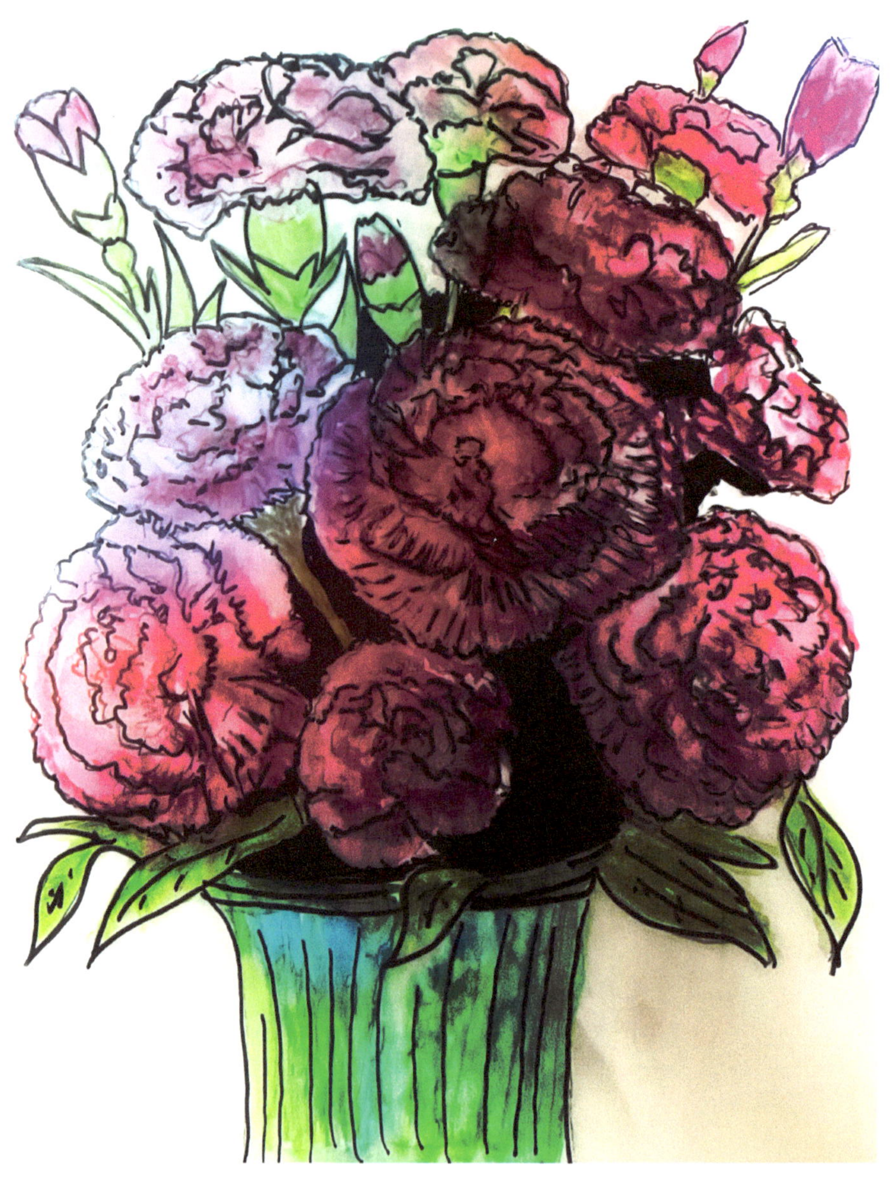

Flowers associated with January include carnations, depending on the colour they can represent purity and luck, gratitude and maternal love, deep affection and admiration, all of which can be welcoming within the home. In addition to carnations, snowdrops are also considered a flower for January, as they are some of the first flowers to bloom at the start of the year, often pushing through snow and frozen ground. Snowdrops symbolise hope and promise of renewal as they mark the transistion from Winter to Spring.

In January we see the Full *Wolf Moon*, this comes from the association with how wolves were often heard howling during cold January nights. It was thought this behaviour was due to wolves communicating to search for food which reinforced pack bonds during the harsh Winter months when food was scarce.

The Wolf Moon usually appears in mid to late January, depending on the year. Like any full moon, it appears fully illuminated due to the alignment of the Earth between the sun and the moon.

It is often seen as a time for reflection and preparation for the year ahead, with various traditions and cultural stories tied to it. Within astrology, the January Full Moon can have different meanings depending on the zodiac sign it falls in. Typically it highlights themes of introspection, personal growth and resilience, fitting the Wintertime context of facing challenges and pushing through difficulties.

Like other full moons, it can be viewed in the Eastern Sky just after sunset. It often appears larger and more vivid when it is near the horizon due to the *moon illusion,* an optical effect that makes the moon appear larger when it is lower in the sky.

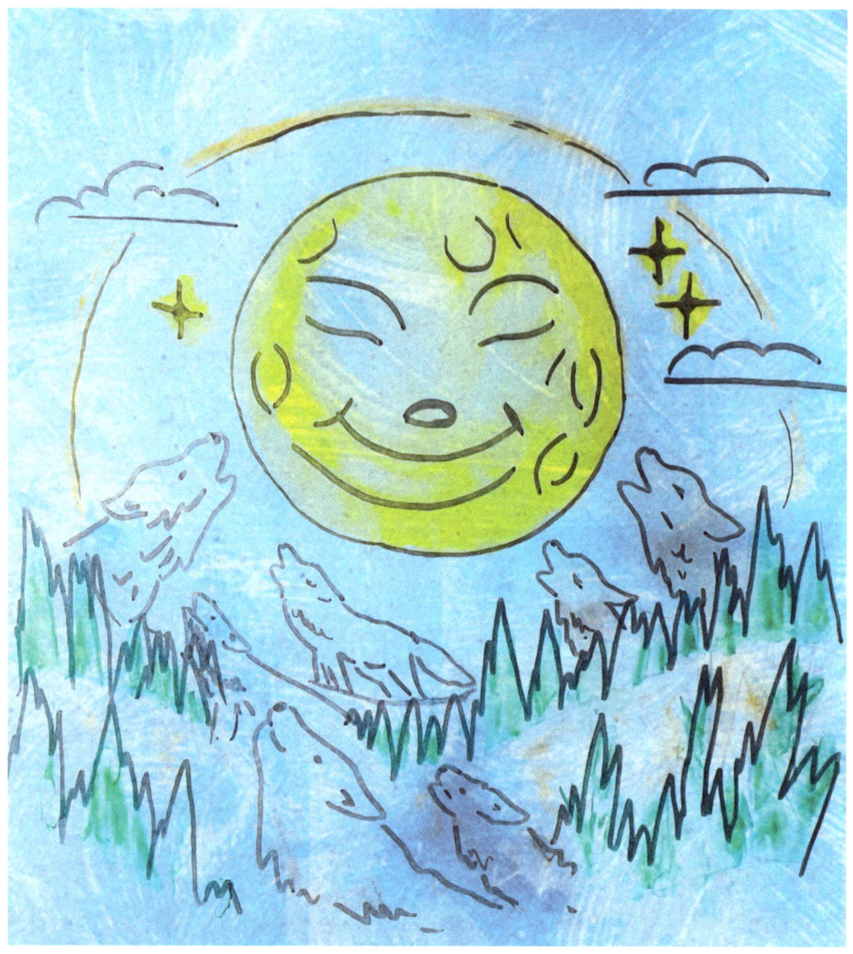

Wolves howl in January for a combination of biological, social and environmental reasons. Some include: the onset of mating season; being territorial animals howling reinforces boundaries as the air is clearer and colder, this allows the sound of their howls travel further as they need to maintain contact when moving through large expanses.

Comfort From A Glow

The evening falls with whispers soft,
A fire crackles, rising aloft.
My saucepan hums with herbs divine,
In my cozy nook, I draw the line.

Between the worlds of night and day,
A candle guides the ancient way,
Mug of spice, a swirl of steam,
In this home, I weave my dream.

Lanterns lit, a woven shawl,
Spells of comfort, that I recall.
Binding peace with gentle words,
With every chant, my soul is stirred.

Here I rest, in sacred light,
Hygge magick, warm and bright,
Each card placed, each sigil drawn,
Holds the glow before the dawn.

New Beginnings Spell

Purpose: Set intentions for the year.

Ingredients: White candle, piece of paper, pen and rosemary.

Instructions: Light the candle and write down your goals for the year. Burn the paper in the flame while visualising those intentions manifesting. Sprinkle the rosemary around the candle for clarity and protection.

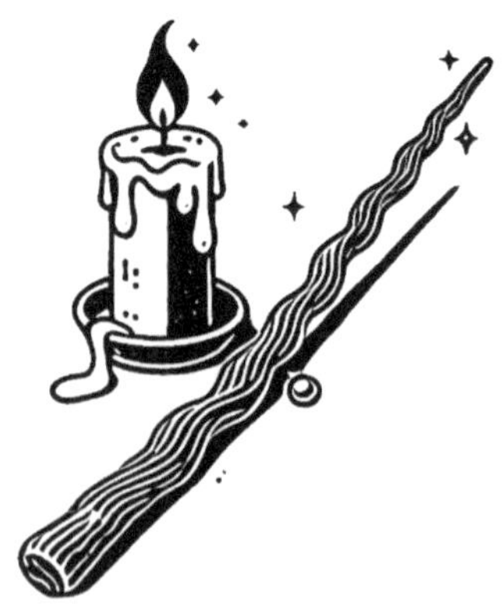

2

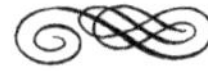

February

February wakes with a tender sigh,
As new green shoots reach for the sky,
Beneath the frost, the earth takes heed,
Whispers of Spring in every seed.

Through Winter's grip, the garden stirs,
Tiny leaves and buds emerge,
With each small sprout, hope softly grows,
The quiet promise nature shows.

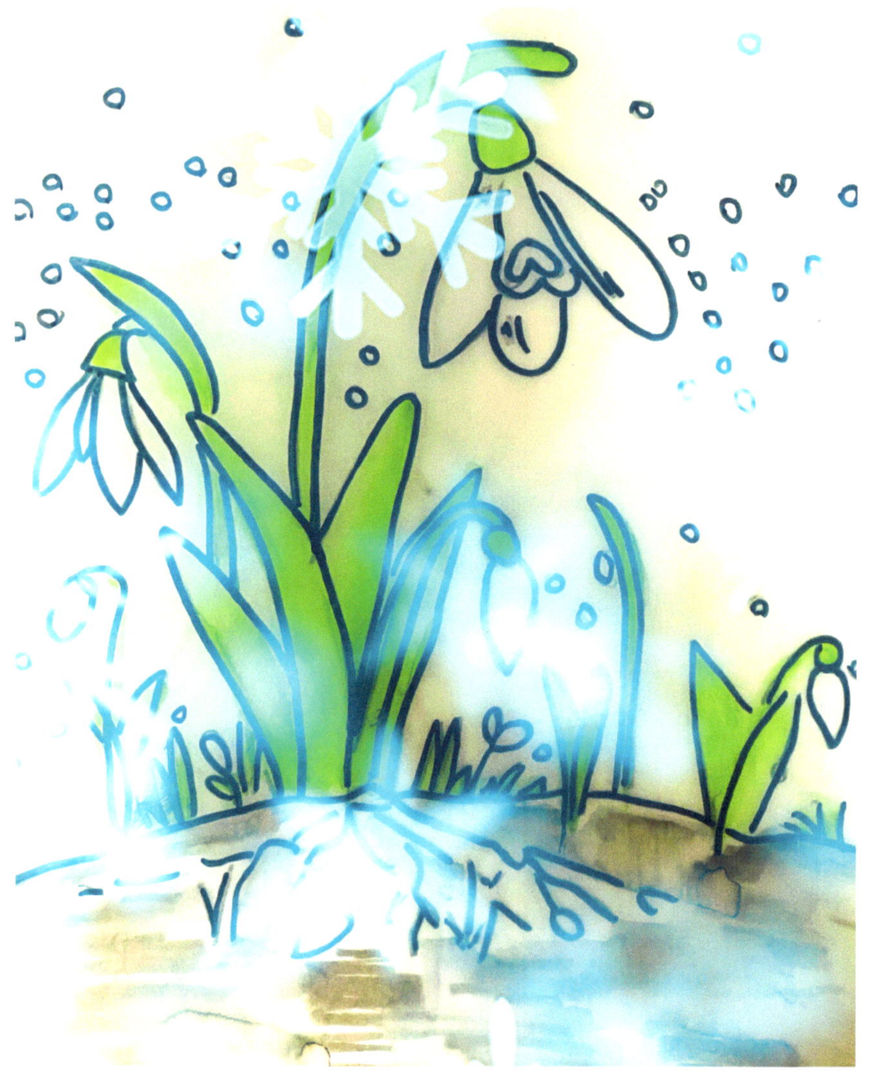

Snowdrops are native to Europe and the Middle East, but have been widely naturalised in other regions, particulary in parts of North America. They have delicate white flowers which are bell-shaped, with three inner petals surrounded by three larger outer petals. All parts of the snowdrop are toxic if they're ingested, containing alkaloids that can be harmful to both pets and humans, but pose no risk if they are simply kept growing from the ground. Snowdrops can still be seen throughout February due to their emergence through the snow, symbolising hope, purity and the promise of Spring.

The month of February has a few associated flowers. Violets symbolise modesty, loyalty and spritual wisdom. Violets can be used in February rituals that focus on love and rememberance. Primroses represent youth and new beginnings. Primroses are a flower tied to energies of February and the Pagan tradition of Imbolc. We mustn't forget the Crocus. The Crocus is often seen as a herald of Spring and symbolises cheerfulness and joy. Croci are radiant when welcomed into the house, with their splash of colour and sweet scent.

February is the month for purification, renewal and preparation for the coming Spring. The start of February marks the half-way point between the Winter Solstice and Spring Equinox. It is around this time that we begin to notice the warmth of the sun returning and the lighter nights and lengthening days return.

This time of year is a good time to start clearing out the old and making way for the new - physically, mentally and spiritually. February is a popular time for purification and cleansing. The definition of Spring cleaning! Some people use herbs like sage or cedar to smudge their houses, whereas others may use salt water or sweeping to sweep the old energy out to welcome in the new.

Crystals associated with February are Amethyst, Moonstone, Clear Quartz, Selenite and Citrine, all of which can be used for personal intention, purification, balance and grounding and meditative practice.

February is also the time to plan gardens or symbolically plant seeds and intentions for the coming year. Since February is a quiet, introspective time, meditation focusing on personal growth, renewal and clarity is powerful. Consider journalling any life lessons you have learnt over the winter months and how you wish to move forwards noting the strength you have displayed to get through them.

As much as we're looking forwards into the warmer days ahead, it is still a time where we are in need of comfort. Pull out your favourite blankets to wrap around yourself whilst curled up on the sofa after a long day to promote well-being.

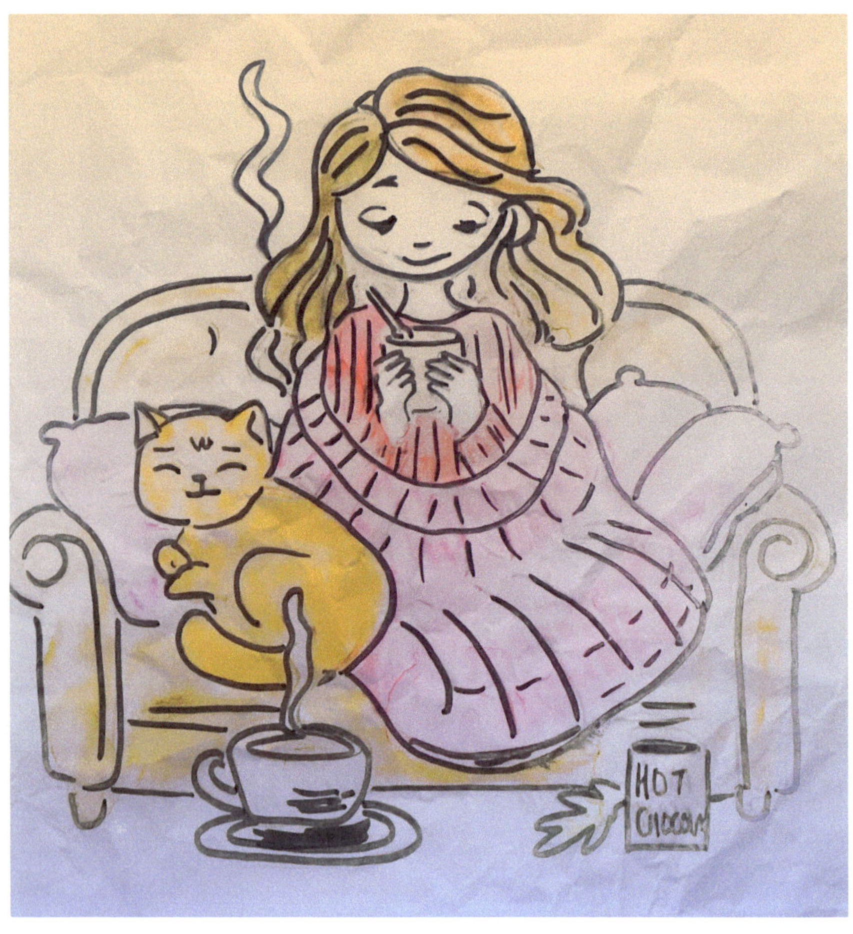

Warm Hearth Whispers

Logs crackle in the hearth's embrace,
Filling the room with an amber trace,
I run my fingers along aged wood,
Where tales of old are understood,

A cat curls close, eyes of jade,
A silent keeper in this charmed parade.
The air is thick with spice and lore,
A hygge witches quiet score,

Blanket forts and woven dreams,
Stitch together my magick schemes,
Each corner, a story, each wall, a wand,
Guarding secrets I've adorned,

Soft chants flow in rhythmic time,
Blending life's pulse, with the divine,
In this space, no shadows bite,
Only warmth and the tender light.

Self Love Bath Ritual

Purpose: Cultivate self-love and healing.

Ingredients: Rose petals, pink himalayan salt, rose quartz and lavender essential oil.

Instructions: Fill a bath with warm water and add the ingredients. Place the rose quartz nearby or in the water. As you soak, repeat affirmations of self-love and let the warmth fill you with positive energy.

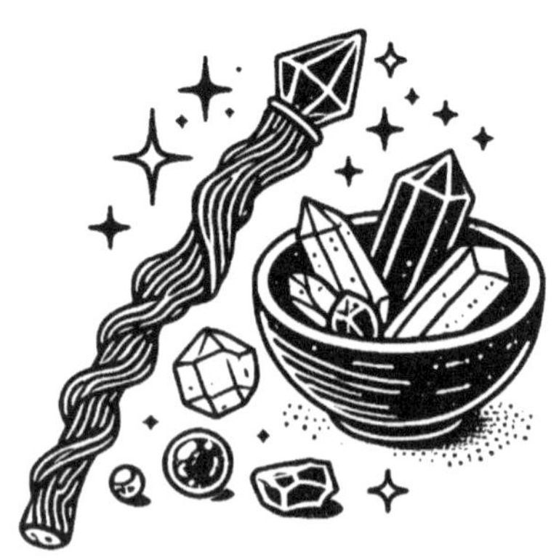

3

March

March arrives with a full moon's gleam,
Birds singing sweet in the morning's beam,
Their calls a sign, the season turns.
As Winter's cold no longer yearns,

With windows wide, the fresh air flows,
Spring cleaning starts as sunlight glows,
Dust is swept and cobwebs fly,
The house reborn beneath the sky.

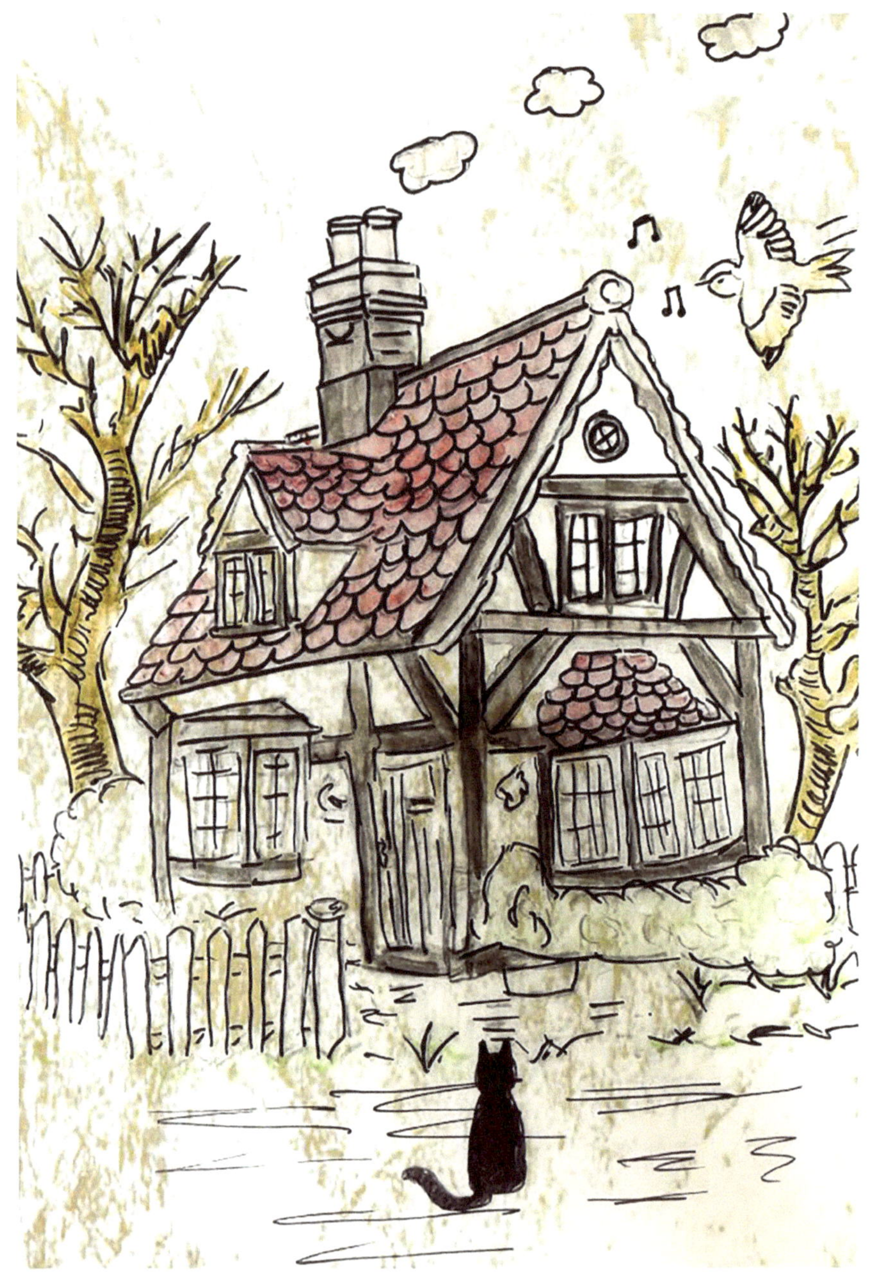

March is a powerful month full of tradition rich in symbolism and seasonal celebrations. March represents the awakening of life after the dormancy of Winter. It embodies growth, rebirth and the return of light and warmth. Taking mindful walks to observe the sign of Spring - new buds, returning animals and greening plants - is common practice for grounding and attuning with nature's cycles. Leave offerings such as birdseed or water out in nature to thank the Earth for its renewal and support the return of wildlife.

Welcome in positive vibrations into the home with clear and new energy that March brings. Green Aventurine is associated with luck and ambundance, this crystal can be used to encourage prosperity. Aquamarine, the birthstone of March symbolises clarity, calmness and renewal. It can promote emotional healing. Moonstone can be used as it connects deeply with the energy and phases of the moon to enhance it's power.

March plays a significant part in the year as the Spring equinox takes place around 20th or 21st. It marks the perfect time for balance bewteen day and night, symbolising equality and transition from the dark half of the year to the light half. The Spring equinox occurs when the sun crosses the celestial equator, resulting in nearly equal hours of daylight and night. This event heralds the official start of Spring in the Northern Hemisphere. The symbolism to the equinox represents balance and harmony. It's a time when energies of light and dark, masculine and feminine and internal reflection and outward growth are in equilibrium.

Decorating homes with symbols of Spring is common practice, spring flowers, eggs and green branches to invite the seasons rejuveating energy. Planting seeds in gardens and pots can symbolise the sowing of dreams and goals for the coming season and year.

March lends the opportunity to watch some beautiful sunrises which can aid well-being. March is all about transistion, rejuvination and preparing for new begininnings. By honouring its energy through rituals, natural observation and symbolism, you can harness its revitilising power to welcome in Spring.

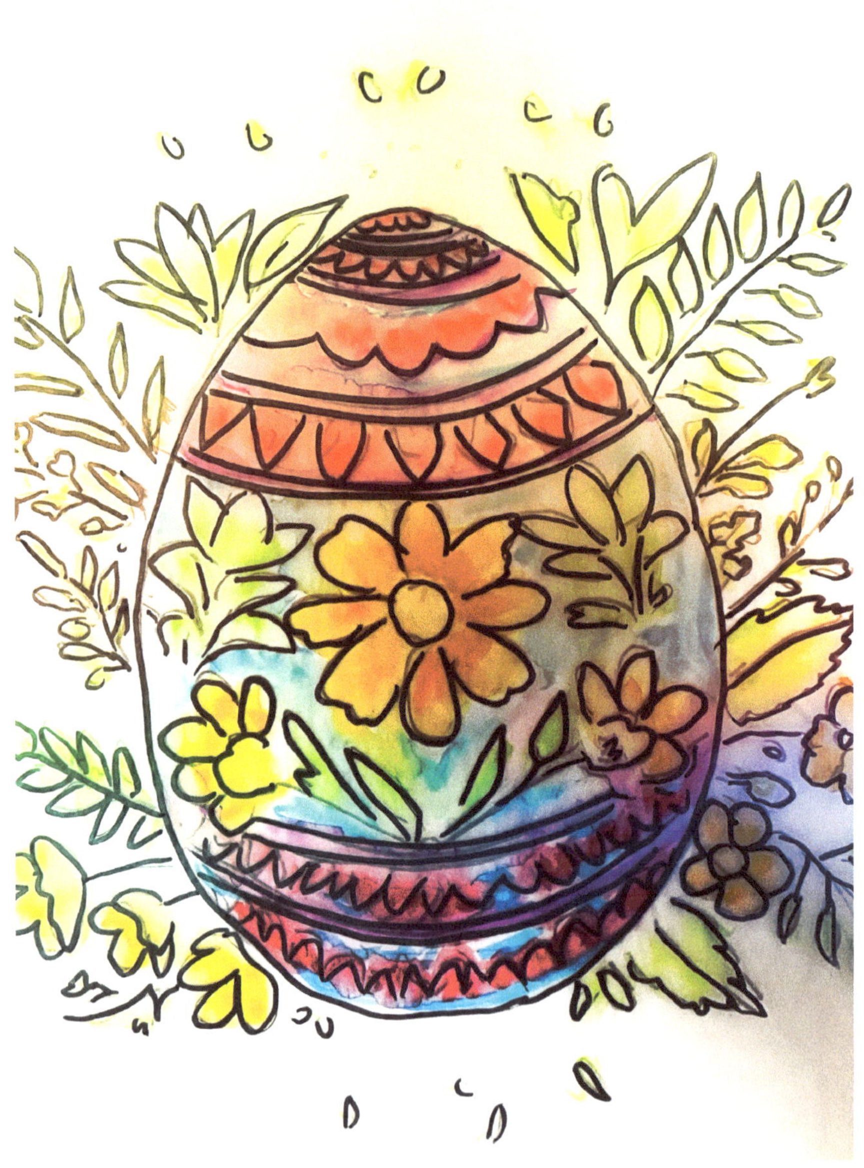

Spring Equinox

Date: Around March 20th.

Significance: Symbolising renewal, fertility and the return of light after darkness.

Themes: Rebirth, renewal and balance. The Spring Equinox marks the end of Winter and the arrival of Spring, when the earth awakens and life blooms again.

Common Rituals and celebrations: Planting seeds, literally and figuratively as it represents growing season. Spring cleaning as it is a time to cleanse and rejuvenate your home with fresh energy. Decorating eggs is a a traditonal activity. Taking walks within nature, soaking in a salt bath and eating nourishing homemade foods to boost your body after a long winter.

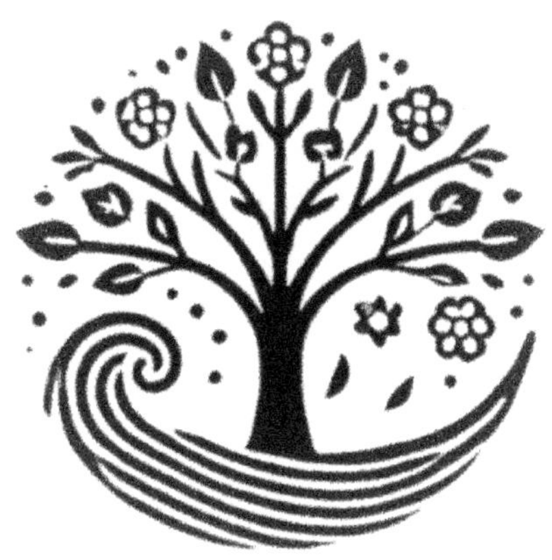

Lanterns and Laughter

Lanterns hang like stars inside,
Glowing with a humble, honest pride,
Amber flames in glassy shells,
Hold the charm of endless spells,

From my window, frost designs,
Fractals drawn in secret signs,
I sip my drink, spiced and sweet,
The nights enchantment at my feet,

There's magick in this simple state,
A life unrushed, a gentle fate,
The clock is hushed, the world is still,
Time bends to a witches will,

I weave my peace, my house-bound art,
Where every glimmer warms my heart,
In the flicker's dance, my spirit sings,
Of home, of hope and quiet things.

The Woven Spell

Knit blankets drape across my knees,
A window framed by darkened trees,
Outside, frost bites, the winds may hiss,
But it's here where I find succoured bliss,

Teapots brim with brewed delight,
Chamomile dreams on a winter's night,
Incense curls in a silken dance,
Casting spells of happenstance,

A witches wand, carved and true,
Points to what the heart can do,
Draw in warmth, let shadows play,
Keep all troubles firmly at bay,

The world is loud, harsh, and bold,
But my magick is quiet, subtle and old,
I am the keeper of peace, a flame so small,
That in its presence, chaos will stall.

Spring Renewal Spell

Purpose: Refresh your space and energy.

Ingredients: A green candle, sage or incense and a small potted plant of your choice.

Instructions: Light the green candle and cleanse your space with the sage or incense. Visualise stagnant energy being replaced by fresh, renewing energy. Place the plant in your home as a symbol of growth.

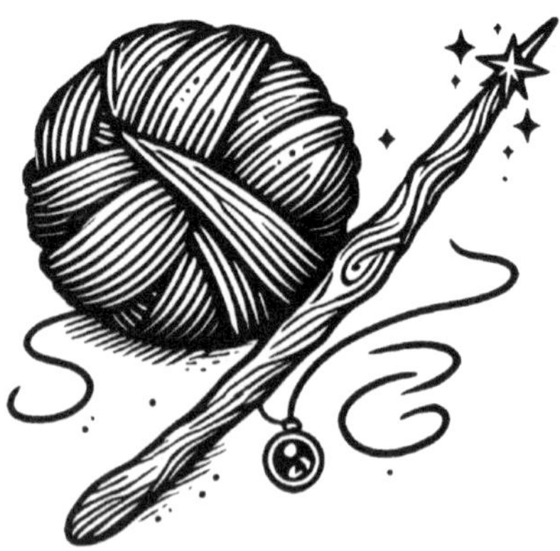

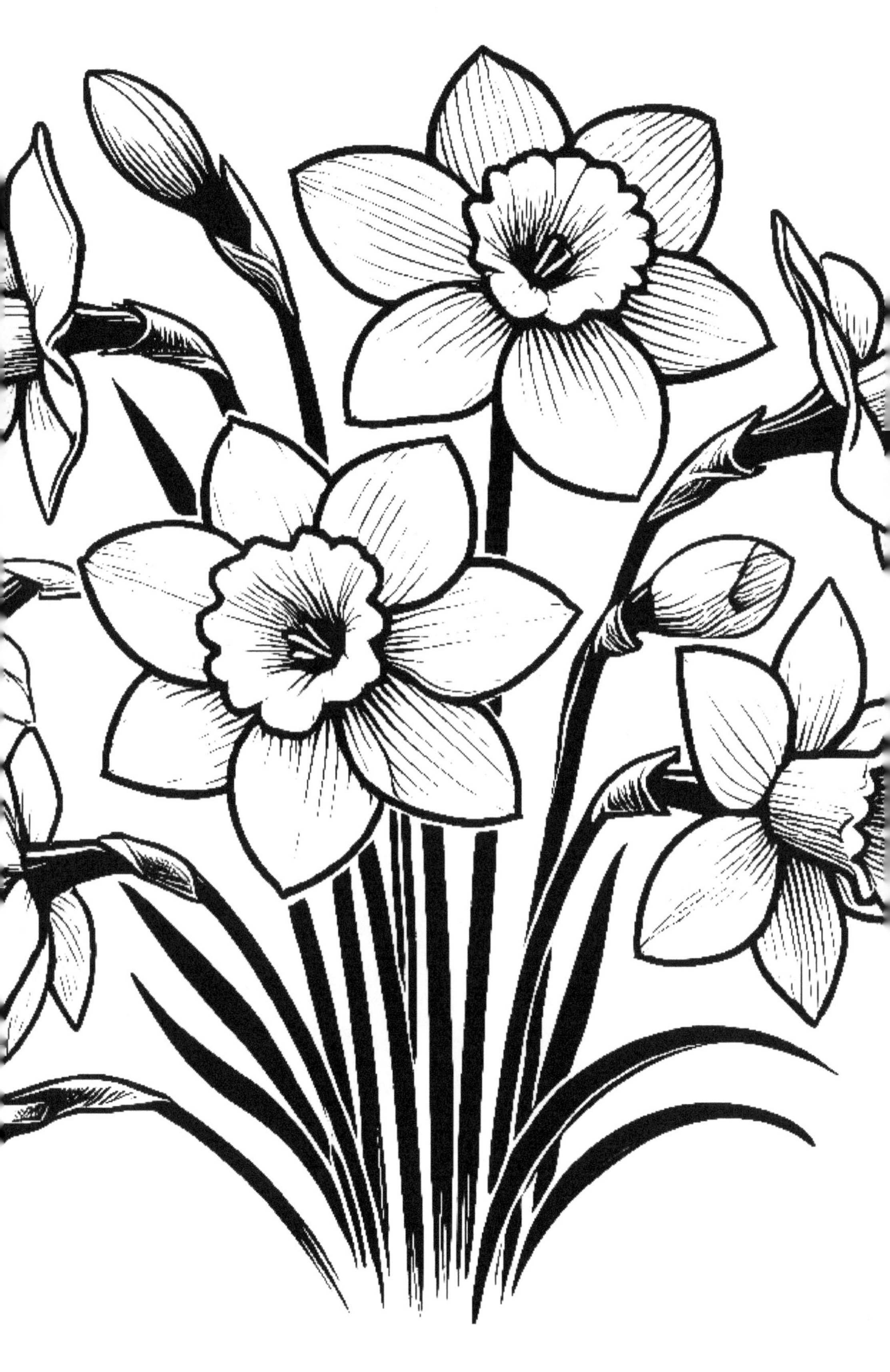

4

April

April blooms in gentle showers,
We wander fields to gather flowers,
Daffodils and tulips bright,
Fill our arms with colours light.

Back at home, the vases brim,
With petals soft on every rim,
The scent of spring now fills the air,
Bringing nature's beauty there.

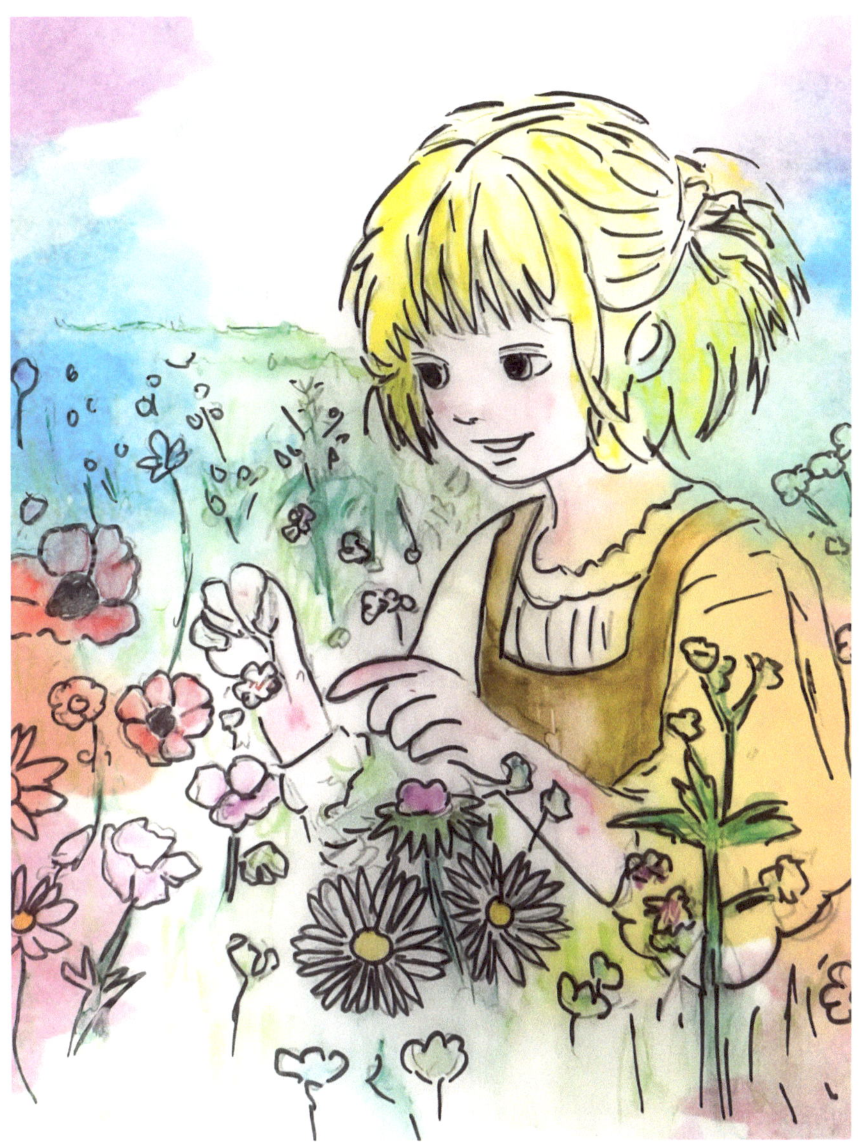

There are many traditions and cultural festivities which occur in April. The end of April marks the coming of the half-way point between the Spring Equinox and the Summer Solstice. April is often associated with fertility, passion and the unity of opposites creating equilibrium within nature. Some Pagan traditions leave offerings such as milk, honey or bread to local spirits in gratitude for the blossoming life of Spring.

Walking in nature really comes into its own in April, wildlife is busy maintaining habitats and their newly born offspring. Buds on the trees, solitary bees are coming out of hibernation and the unmistakable scents of wild garlic amongst blankets of blue bells. April brings the feeling of joy derived from emerging of the harsh stillness of winter.

April is a good time to embark upon new interests and hobbies, using crystals tied to creativity can help focus. Carnelian supports passion, vitality and courage, aventurine, associated with prosperity, abundance and growth, rose quartz linked with love and healing excells at fostering self-care and heart based rituals during this season of growth. Clear Quartz - with its energy amplifying properties - is ideal for the purpose of magnifying ones intentions.

During the month of April we see the Full *Pink Moon.* This epithet does not refer to the moon's colour, but instead draws inspiration from the early bloom of pink pholox flowers native to much of North America.

The moon symbolises rebirth and renewal, aligning with the general theme of growth and blossoming in Spring. Spritually the Pink Full Moon embodies themes of hope, nurturing new beginnings and cultivating relationships. These associations blend natural symbolism and spirtual beliefs making April a month flush in ritual meaning.

Lambing can start as early as December and can extend to June. Lambs are on their feet minutes after birth and can recognise up to fifty other sheep, as well as recognising and several humans. Lambs are very social and form bonds with other lambs and their mothers often displaying playful and curious behaviour which can be observed during this time of year. If you get the chance observing lambs playing, can really enhance your well-being...

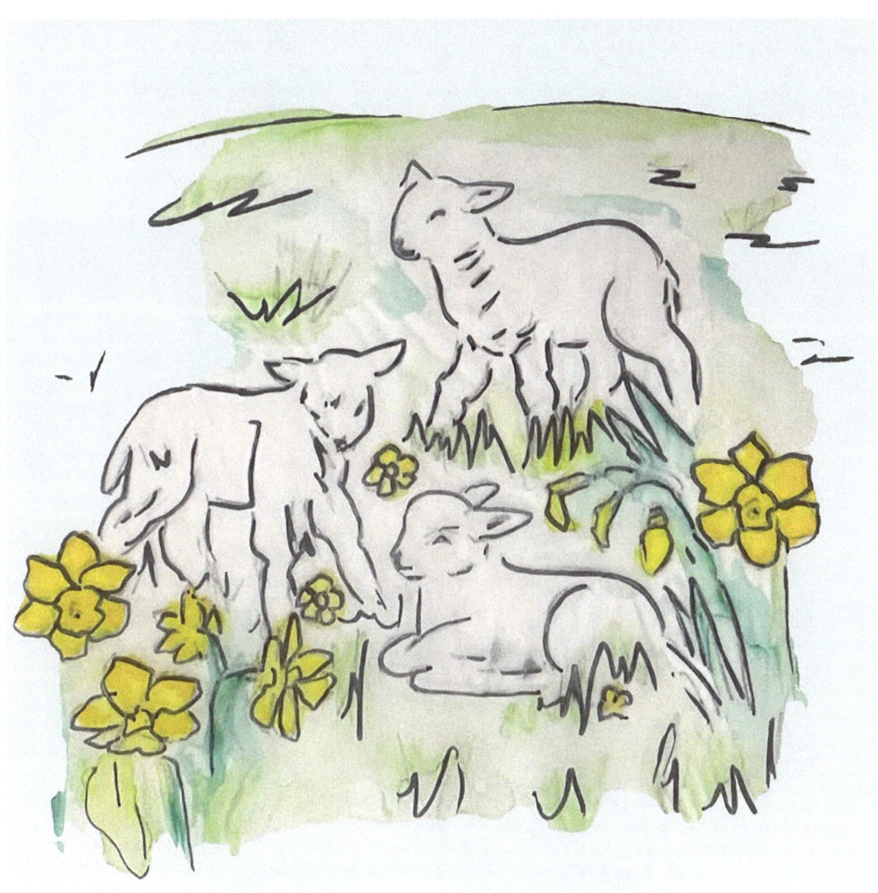

Rain Water Prosperity Spell

Purpose: Attract abundance.

Ingredients: Collected rainwater within a container, a gold coin or pyrite stone and a bowl.

Instructions: On a rainy day, place the coin or pyrite in a bowl and pour rainwater over it.

Say *"As the rain blesses the earth, may prosperity rain down on me"*

Leave the bowl out for a few hours before using the water to sprinkle around your entrance or workplace.

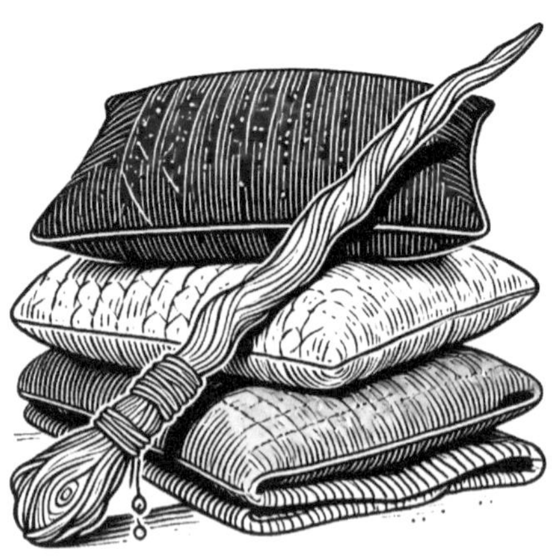

5

May

In May, the garden calls us near,
To plant the seeds of Summer's cheer.
Potatoes, peas, and greens take root,
In the soil we tend, each tiny shoot,

With hands in earth, we work the day,
Nurturing life in gentle May,
The promise of a harvest grows,
In every row our care bestows.

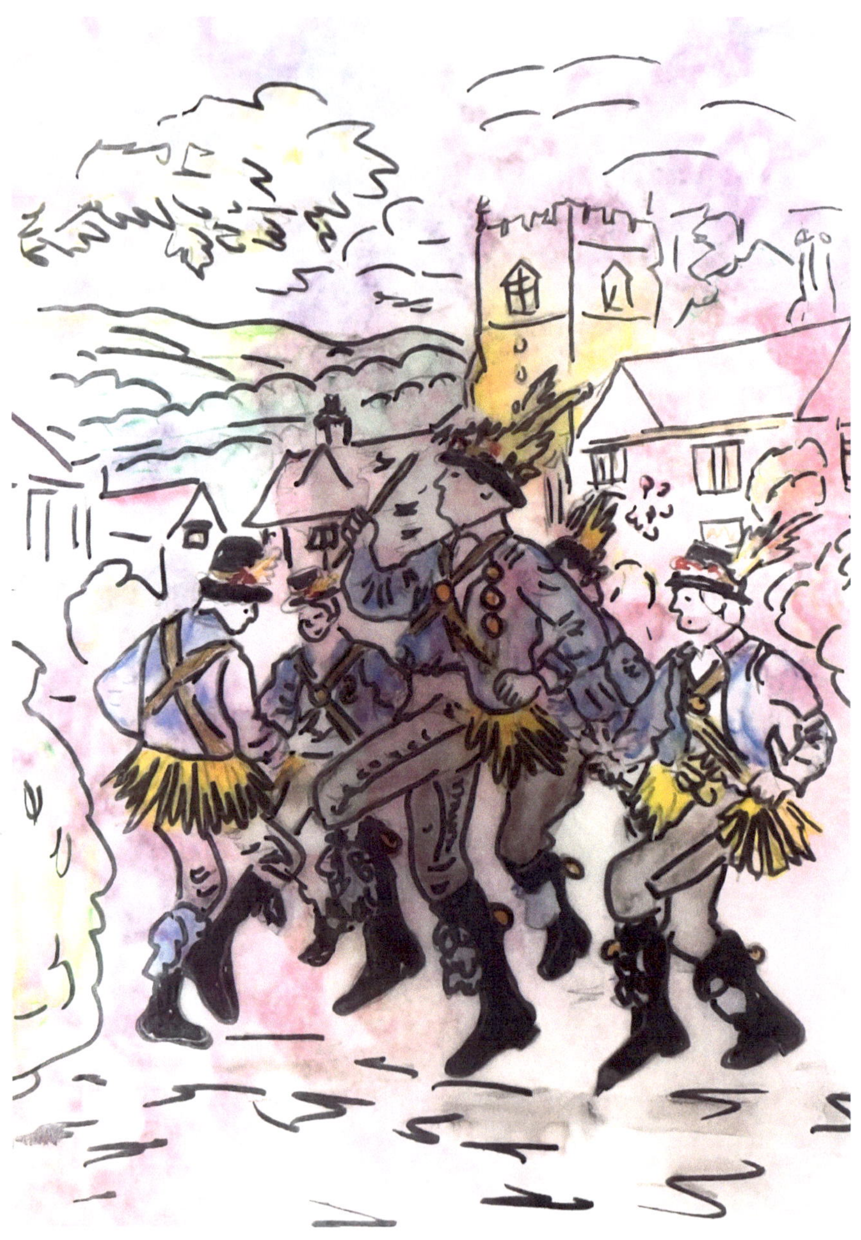

May is filled with celebration as it is the height of Spring and the approach of Summer. It reveres fertility, fire and passion. Across the world there are many traditions consecrated in May. Pagans honour Beltane, by lighting bonfires, circling maypoles, crafting flower crowns and making offerings to nature spirits. Connecting with the blossoming world is an integral part of making the most of May.

May is the time to start decorating your outdoor spaces. Create cosy gardens, balconies or yards. Comfortable seating, soft lighting form a great environment and enjoy the mild evenings.

Seasonal foods are ripe and ready, rhubarb pie or salads with edible seasonal flowers add a touch of comfort and celebration. Decorate your home with nature, by bringing in fresh flowers and greenery to fill your space with life. Engaging in crafts such as wreath and garland making, with collected native materials found on a walk, help nurture a deep impression of connectivity with the time of year.

The full moon in May is known as the Full *Flower Moon* due to the abundance of flora at this time, other names for it have been the full *Milk Moon* or the full *Corn Moon,* which have a farming background and refers to the affluence of milk and corn.

One very special bloom, found at this time of year, is held in high regard amongst many cultures and within folklore: The Hawthorn - otherwise known as the Mayflower. The Hawthorn represents the peak of Spring, hope, fertility and the prosperity of the land. There are many traditional folk customs which you may be lucky to observe around this time. These include morris dancers and fire festivals. It is said that the Legends say the Hawthorn tree is said to be guarded by fairies ready to protect it should the need arise.

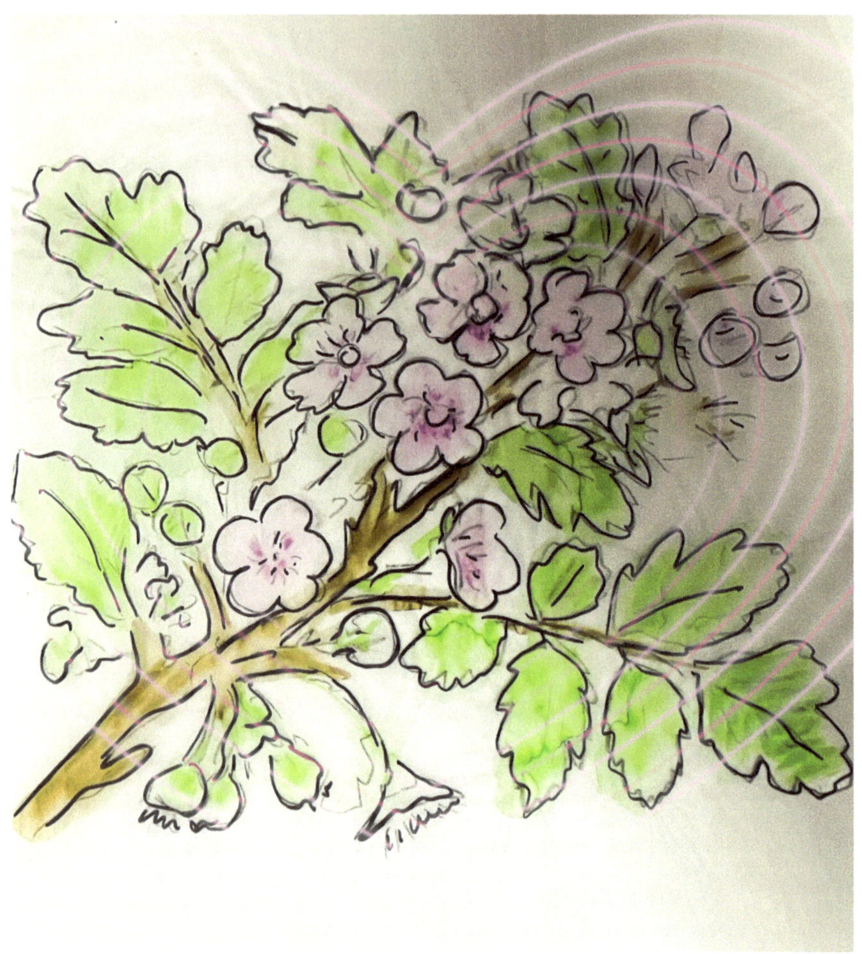

It is one of the most celebrated and sacred trees:
Associated with enchantment, love and protection - delicate five petal blossoms open in May, and with its abundant foliage and thorny branches, its wood is employed for shelter.

The Cosy Enchantress

Woolen socks and fire's light,
Cloak me in the calm of night,
A spell of rest, a charm of dreams,
In this space, all is as it seems.

I light my candles, scent of pine,
For sacred hours when all is mine,
Cards laid out, with whispers shown,
Revealing paths till then unknown,

Biscuits cool upon the rack,
A sweet enchantment, warmth's attack,
Baking is a sacred art,
Every crumb, a piece of heart,

Magick's not always wild and loud,
Sometimes it's nestled in a cloud,
Of shared stories, quilted love,
A simple spell cast from above.

May Flower Crown Ritual

Purpose: Connect with nature and honour the divine feminine.

Ingredients: Fresh flowers such as daises, lavender, lilacs and floral wire or twine.

Instructions: Weave a crown with the flowers while visualising the beauty of the season infusing you with joy and vitality. Wear it during meditation.

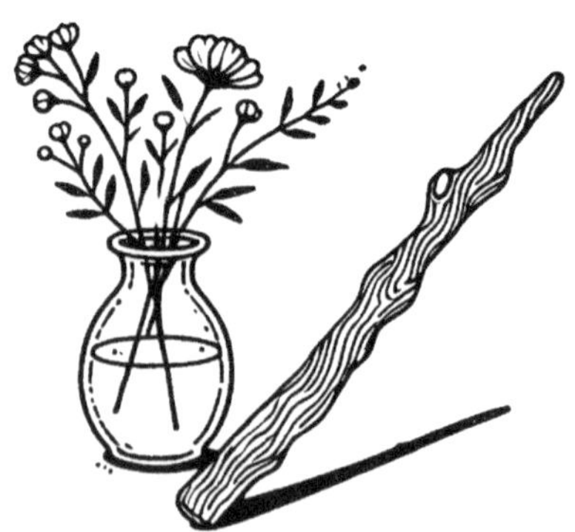

6

June

In June, the sun is warm and bright,
Yet in the kitchen, feels just right,
Flour spills and sugar swirls,
As cakes are baked, sweet treats unfurl.

The scent of vanilla fills the air,
With warmth and comfort everywhere,
Outside, the world in summers bloom,
Inside, we savour cakes' perfume.

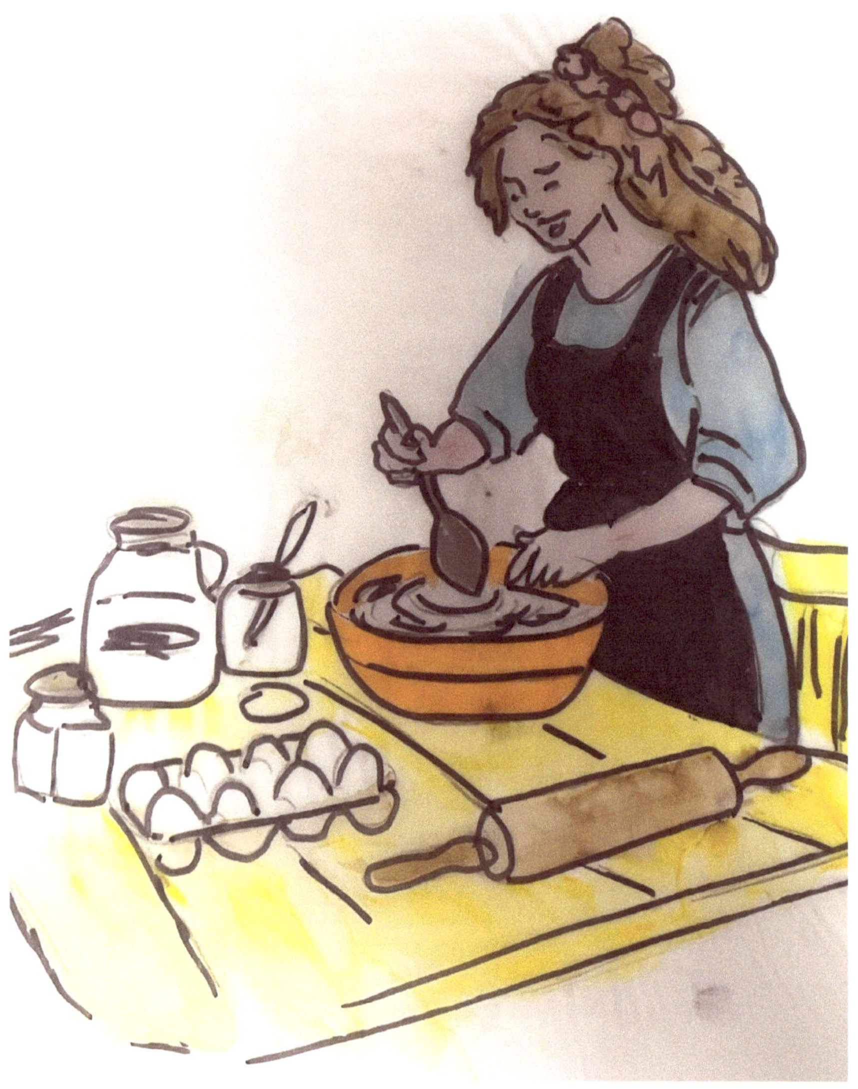

June is associated with the Summer Solstice, also known as Midsummer, a festival honouring the longest day of the year and the peak of solar energy. It is a time to honour plenitude, warmth, potency and the balance bewteen light and darkness. Some traditions acknowledge the vitality of the sun and the fullness of nature's bounty bestowed this month. We celebrate with outdoor gatherings in nature amongst friends and family surrounded by flowers and greenery. We also enjoy picnics with handmade natural food and herbal teas.

Fire rituals can symbolise the sun. They can serve as a focal point for storytelling, singing or quiet reflection. Keeping a journal can help focus on your goals and intentions set earlier in the year.

There are certain flowers which bloom in June, roses represent love, passion and joy. They are often used in Midsummer rituals to signify the fullness of life. Lavender embodies peace, relaxation, and spiritual connection; perfect for creating a hygge atmosphere, as it can be placed in vases or herbal sachets.

Honeysuckle is associated with protection and spritual energy. It can be woven into garlands or wreaths. Peonies represent prosperity and good fortune, their lush full blooms make them ideal for decorating altars or dining tables.

Getting crafty and making flower crowns is a symbolic way of connecting with nature and celebrating the peak of growth, enjoy the early rises with glorious sunrises to perform a meditation soaked in the sun's energy, bathing within its light and drawing in its power for renewal and vitality.

Herb bundles made from rosemary, thyme and sage can cleanse your space or yourself. This aligns with the idea of purification and new beginnings.

Certain crystals can be used in June for the purpose of harvesting the month's energy. Citrine, known for promoting joy, positivity and abundance. Citrine's sunny energy aligns with the power of the solstice and enhances self-confidence and creativity.

Moonstone represents intuition and feminine energy. It is particulary powerful during the solstice for connecting with the cycles of the moon and augmenting wisdom.

Sunstone is associated with leadership and vitality. It clasps the essence of solar energy, making it ideal for the solstice rituals to invigorate and energise the spirit. Tiger Eye helps maintain balance and harmony, grounding the energetic surge that comes from the longest day of the year.

In June the full moon is commonly known as the *Strawberry Moon*, traditionally marking the time of year when this fruit is harvested.

This moon's symbolism is laden with prosperity and acheivement. It is held as a period to reap the benefits of hard work and enjoy the rewards of one's labour. This moon is also often associated with romance and relationships.

It embodies love and connection, making it a good time for strengthening bonds with others or performing romance related rituals.

Combining these practices create a harmonious balance between the high energy of summer and the calming, intimate essence of hygge, blending ritual and comfort for a serene, reflective June celebration.

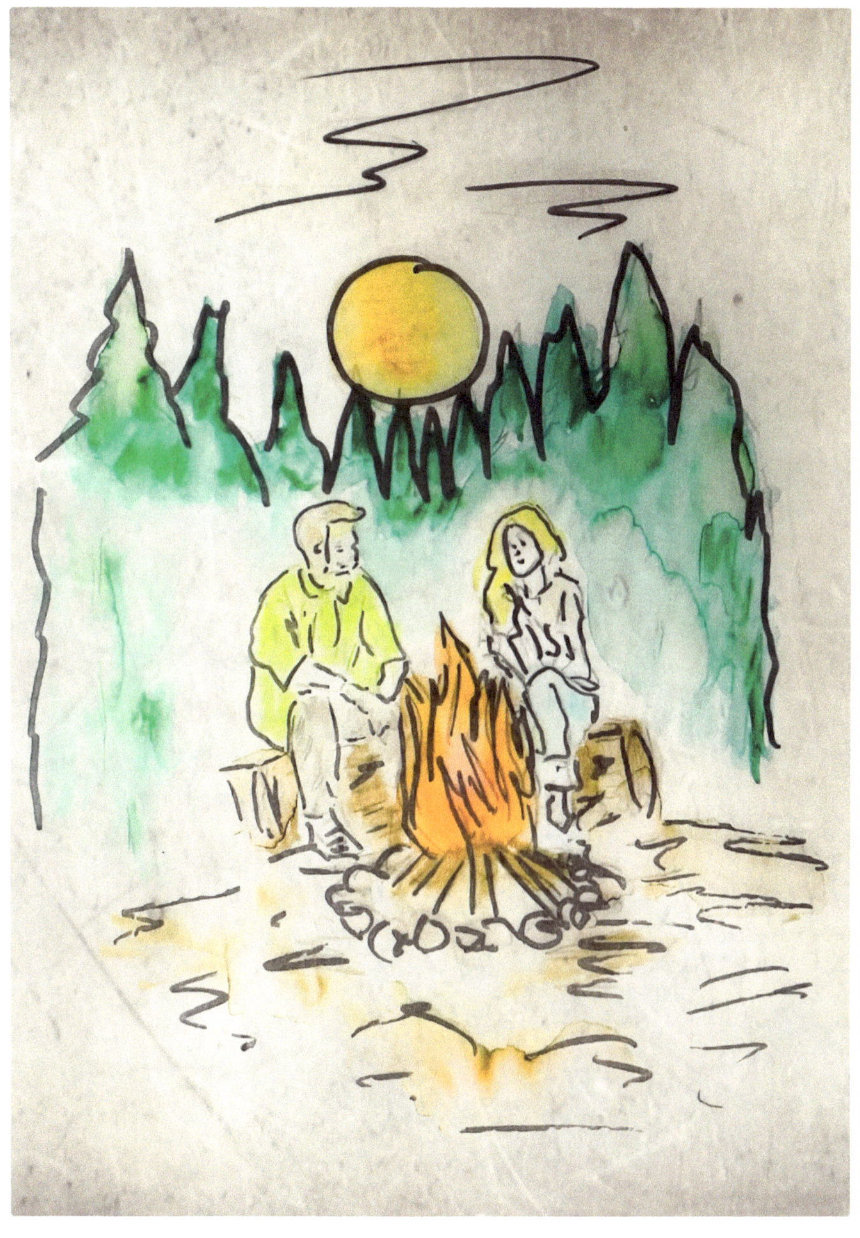

Summer Solstice

Date: Around June 21st.

Significance: The Summer Solstice marks the longest day of the year when the sun reaches its highest point in the sky. This is a celebration of the peak of solar power, wealth and life. It is a time to revel in the bloom of Summer and the nurturing warmth of the sun.

Themes: Power of the sun symbolises vitality, strength and growth, riches and prolificacy and a time when communities dance and gather together.

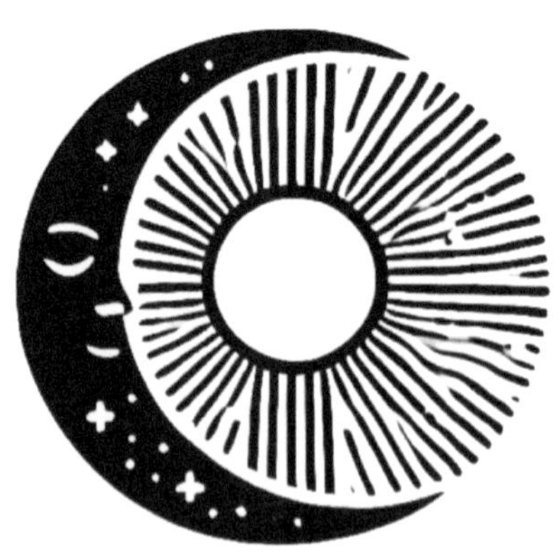

Tea Leaves and Tales

A kettle whistles, sharp and bright,
Against the veil of deep, soft night
The leaves unfurl, a fragant spell,
A story that they yearn to tell,

I cradle the warmth between my hands,
A sacred cup, where time expands,
It's here I find my hidden self,
Amid the books upon the shelf.

Spirits of ancestors linger near,
Their laughter woven into cheer,
They guide my hands with sacred touch,
Reminding me of roots and such,

From crystal bowls to copper rings,
Every small, enchanted thing,
Holds a power, deep and wide,
In this home where dreams reside,

Sun Energy Spell

Purpose: Harness solar energy for vitality.

Ingredients: Yellow candle, sunstone and a piece of orange.

Instructions: Light candle during the day and hold the sunstone in your hand. Eat the orange slowly while visualising the sun's warmth and energy filling your body and mind with positivity and power.

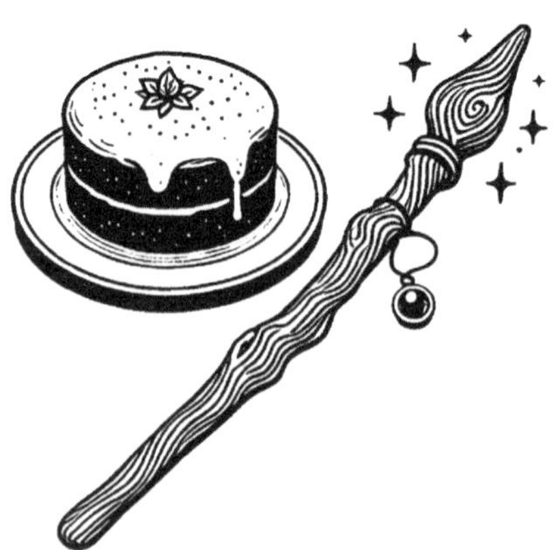

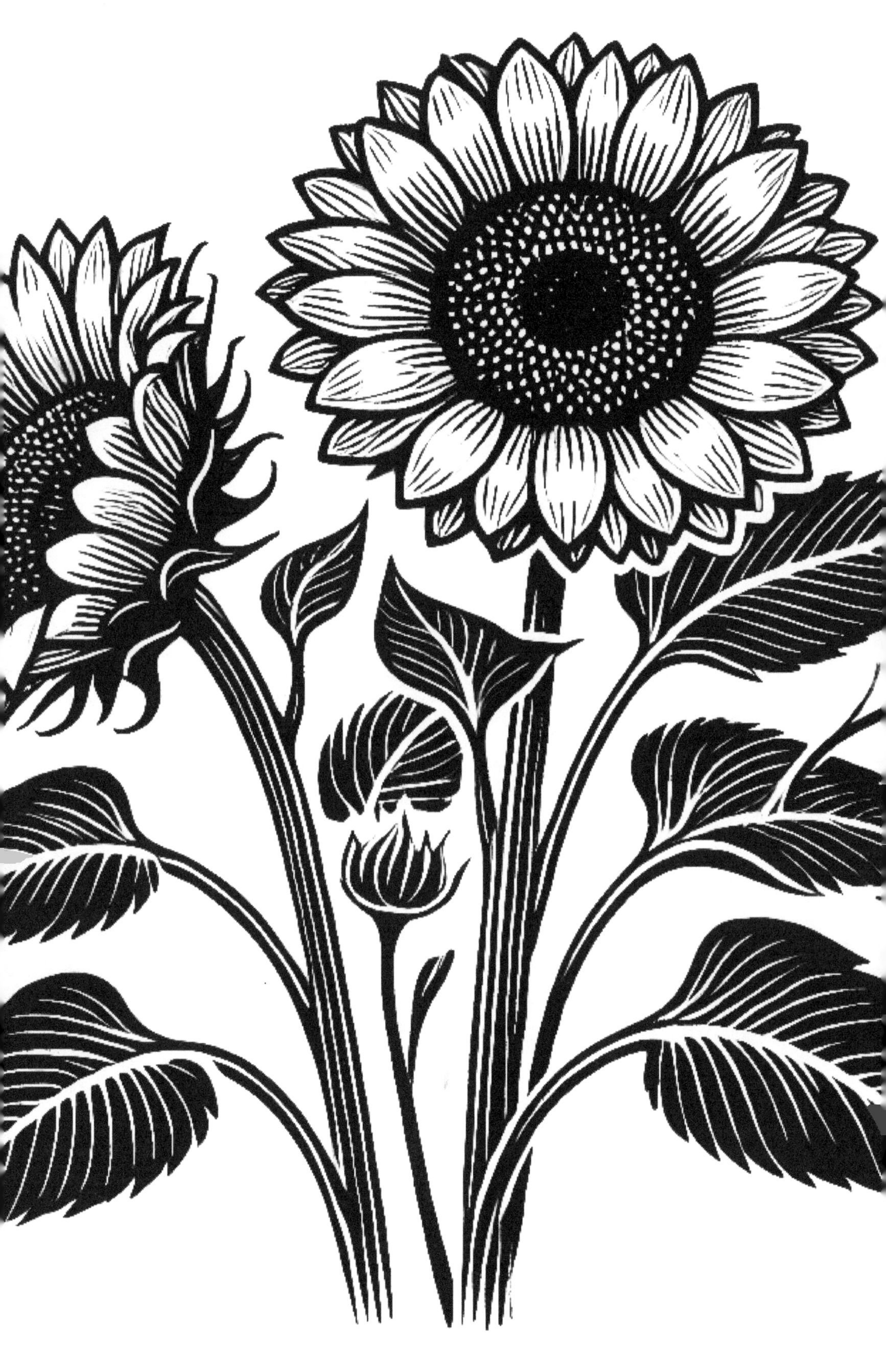

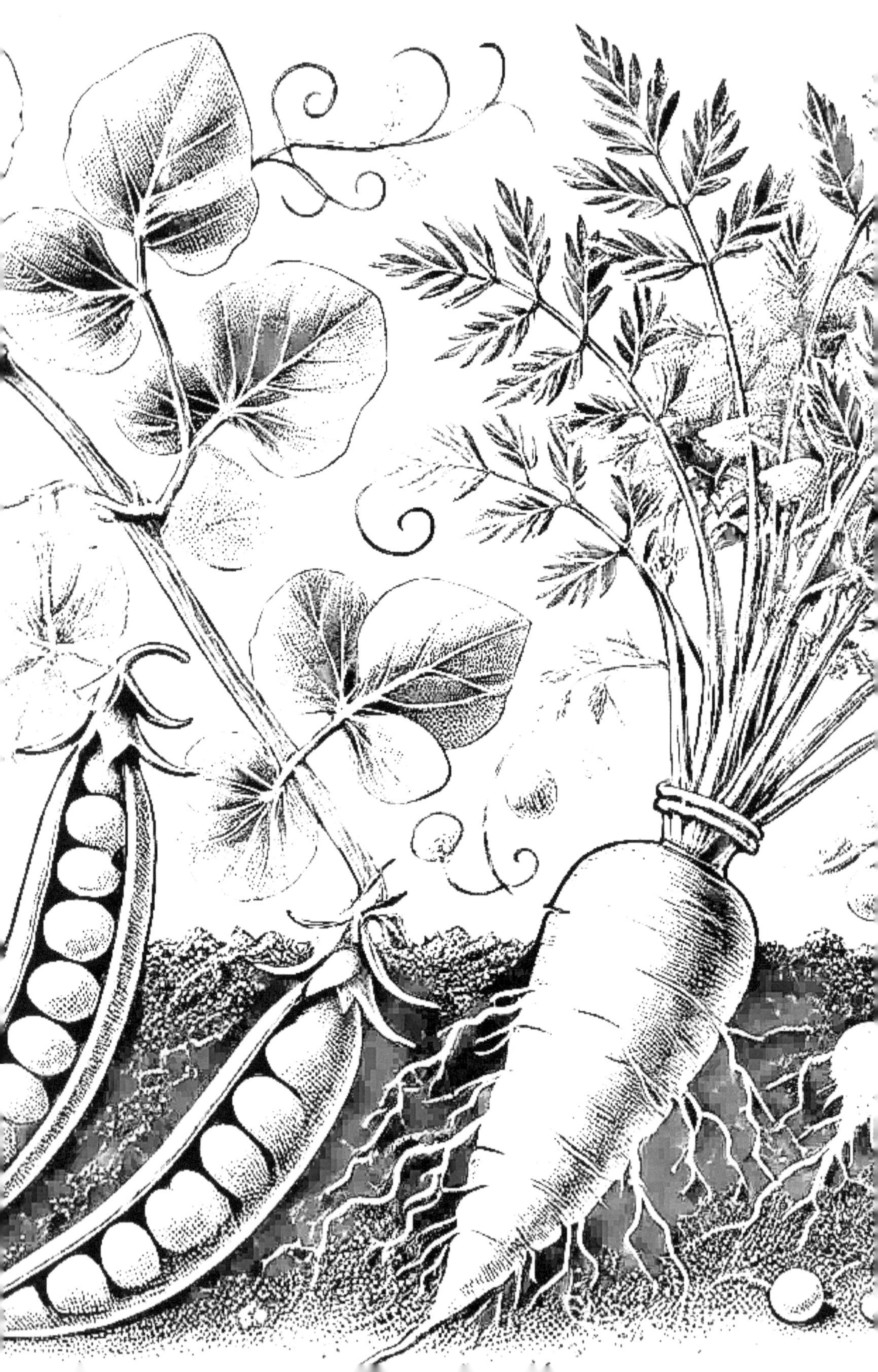

7

July

July arrives with harvests grace,
The garden yields its vibrant space,
We gather peas and carrots sweet,
The first fresh vegetables we have to eat,

In the kitchen, pots gently steam,
A summer soup, a quiet dream,
From earth to bowl, the seasons prize,
In every spoon, the garden lies.

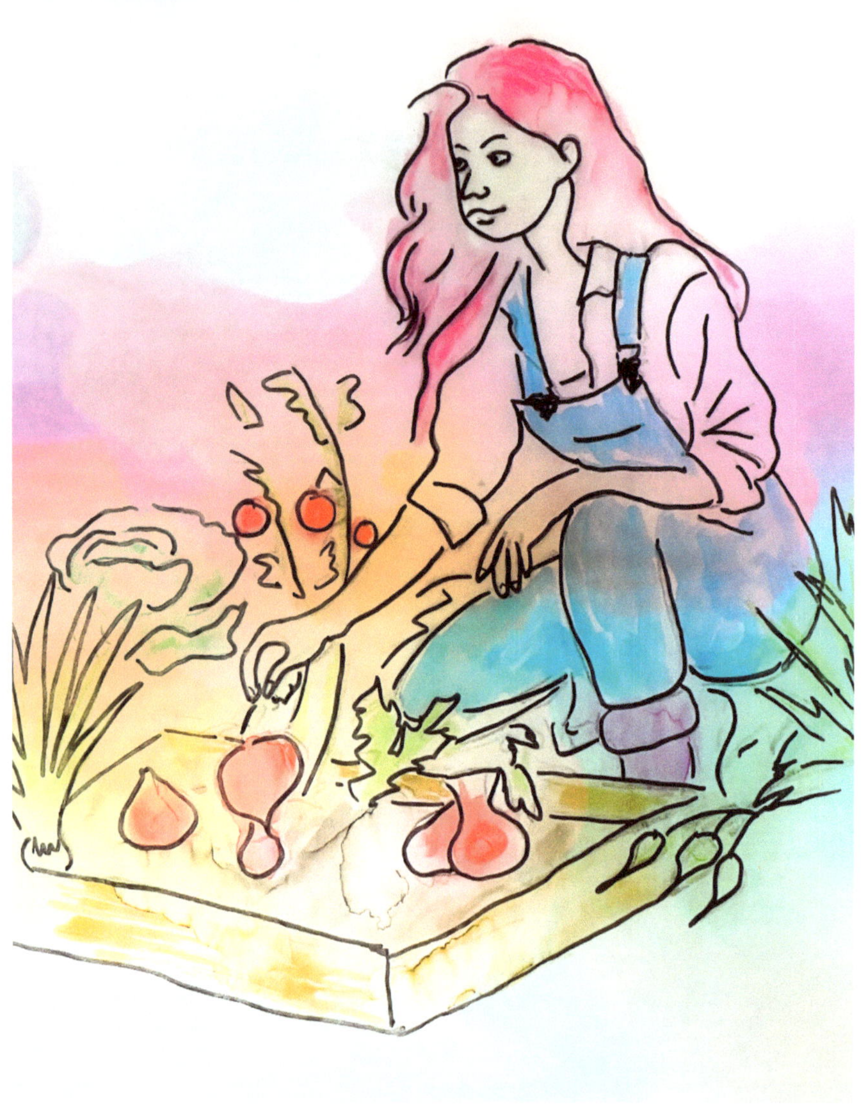

July is a time to appreciate the plenitude of nature, as the harvest season begins in many parts of the world. The energy is vibrant and full of life, perfect for reflecting on personal growth, gratitude and the relationships we nurture. July clebrations focus on comfort, simplicity and synergy with nature. Enjoy seasonal fruits, breads and Summery dishes with family and friends. Decorate the home with wildflowers and herbs. A picnic with comfortable cushions, light blankets and woven baskets filled with homemade food exemplifes a hygge vibe.

Flowers associated with July include the Sunflower, which represents loyalty, strength, and happiness. Their bright appearance can bring positive energy into any space. Water-lillies symbolise peace and purity, whilst daisies embody innocence; they can be woven into garlands or placed in vases to cstablish a cheerful environment. Gathering Summer herbs to produce infusions or teas is a pleasent method by which to connect to July's joys.

Lavender Tea Recipe

Ingredients:

- 1 tbsp dried lavender buds
- 2 cups of water
- Honey or Lemon to taste (optional)

Instructions:

- Bring 2 cups of water to boil.
- Add the dried lavender buds to teapot or infuser.
- Pour boiling water over the lavender buds and let it steep for five/ten minutes.
- Strain the tea into cups
- Sweeten with honey if desired
- Enjoy a warm and soothing experience

Carnelion is a stone encompassing vitality, motivation and creativity. It boosts energy and exudes joy, making it perfect for summer rituals. Ruby is known for its deep red hue which symbolises passion, strength and love. It enhances your life force and encourages confidence. Rose Quartz amplifies love and harmony. It is ideal for rituals that focus on nurturing relationships and promoting peace. Clear quartz strenghtens intentions and purifies energy. It is an excellent companion stone, which can be charged under the July sun or the full moon, which is termed the *Buck Moon,* named for the time of year when male deer grow their antlers. This lunar phase is associated with growth, strength and preparation for the future, as it invites reflection on past actions and encourages setting goals for the coming months. Manifestation ceremonies under the Buck Moon can be powerful. Write down intentions for upcoming months on pieces of paper and place them in a fireproof dish. Light a small candle and let the flame pass over the papaer safely, symbolising the ignition of your goals.

Establish a cosy space using scented candles with aromas such as vanilla, citrus or floral notes to evoke warmth and comfort. Soft textiles and blankets in nooks where you can relax, read or meditate embrace a cosy vibe.

Celebrate July: be mindful of your connection to the earth and embrace the warmth of the season and grasp elements of summer; this can be both heartwarming and fulfilling.

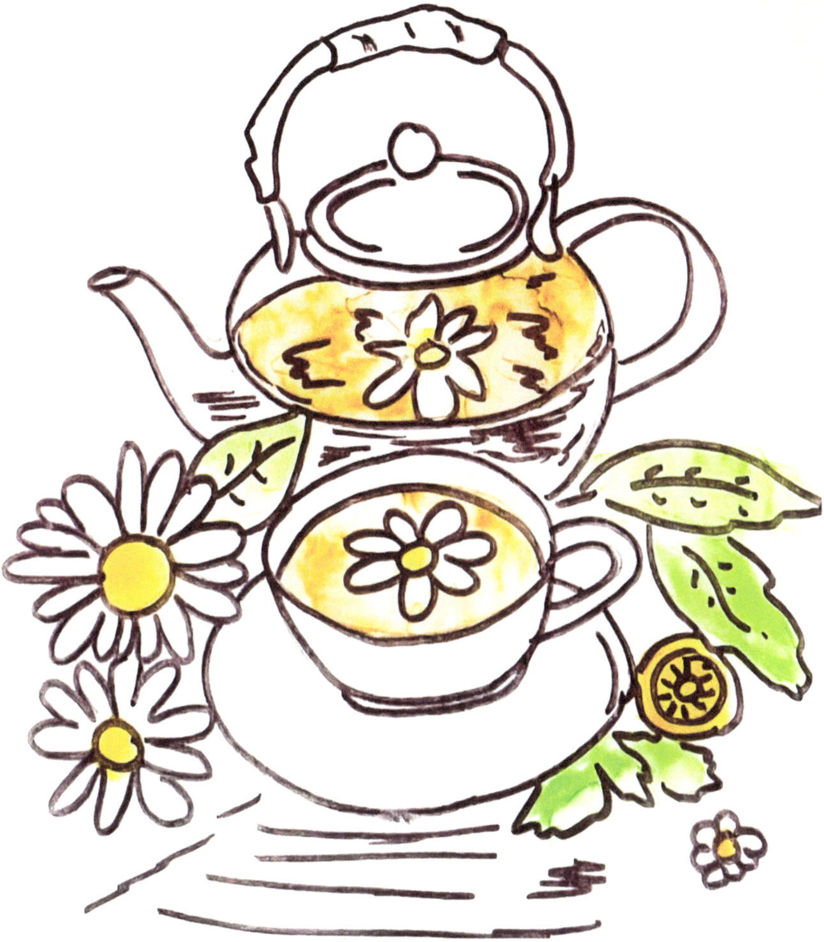

Using the same recipe format as the Lavender tea, you can alternate herbs around to support your own health and well-being to make fresh herbal teas to support your needs.

Quiet Magick

Beneath the silver of the moon,
A song that sings a soothing tune,
The house creaks as it settles down,
In a quilt of stars, my magicks crown,

An old cat purrs, secure and grey,
He sits in tune with my spirits play,
From midnight oil to ink and feather,
I conjur warmth, despite the weather.

Spells of laughter, bound in twine,
Are gifts of mine, simple and fine,
A home that holds no fear or fray,
A beacon to those who lose their way,

So here I sit, a woman so mild,
With charms both fierce and still beguiled,
No thunder's clash or tempest wild,
Just comfort, cosiness, reconcilled.

Summer Protection Spell

Purpose: Protect against negative energies.

Ingredients: Seashells, salt and a blue candle.

Instructions: Create a circle using seashells and salt. Sit inside the circle and light the blue candle. Visualise a barrier of light around you, guarding you against negativity.

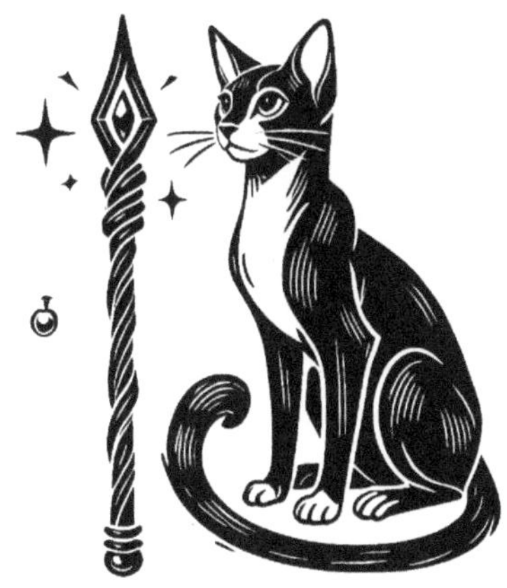

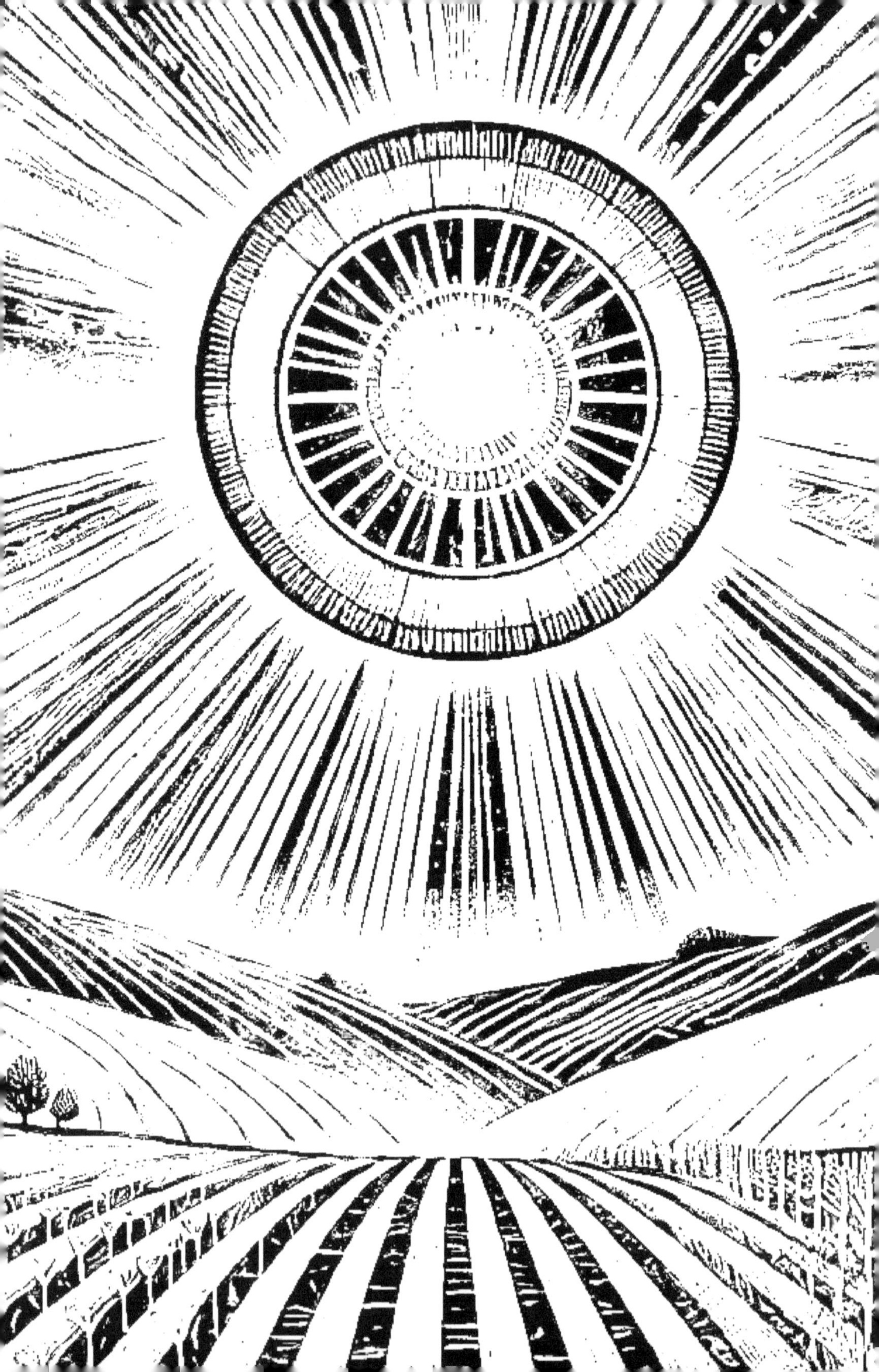

8

August

In August's warmth, I find my place,
A shaded spot, a quiet space,
With book in hand, the hours drift,
Each page a gentle summer gift,

The cat beside me, basking slow,
In golden rays, a lazy glow,
The golden hums, the world at ease,
In August's sun, we share the peace.

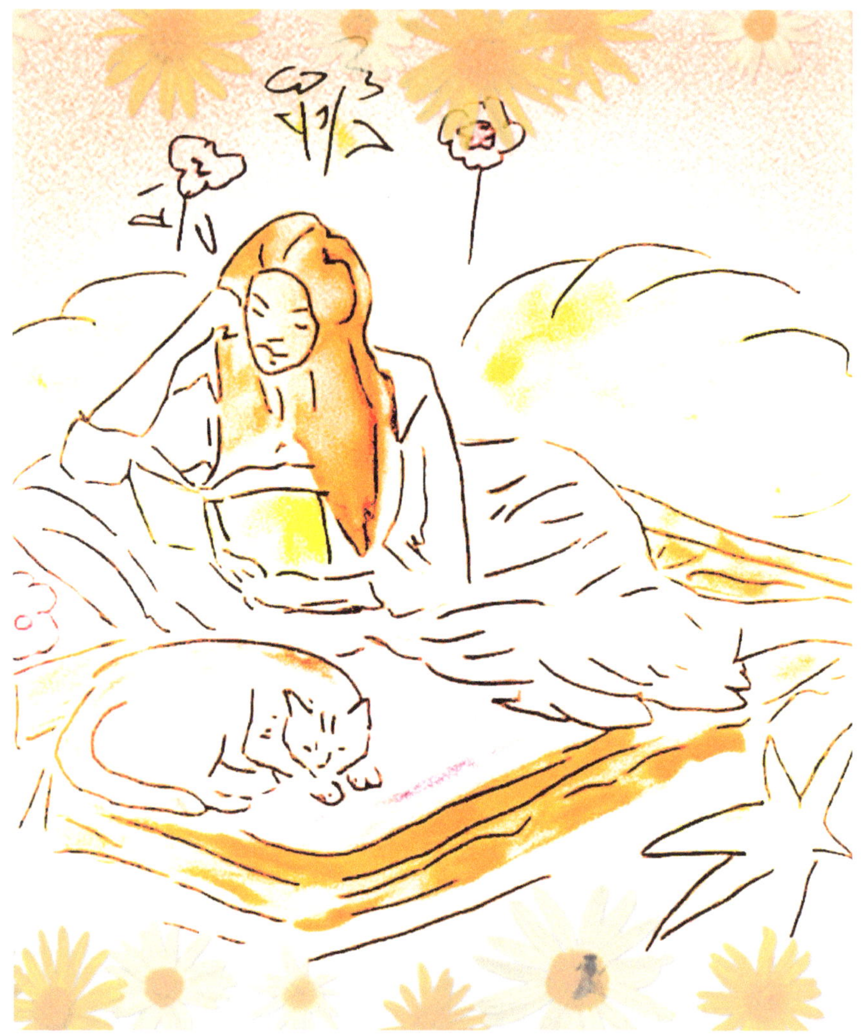

August holds significant meaning as it marks the transition from the height of Summer towards the early signs of Autumn. August is a time for gratitude, abundance and preparation. We reflect on personal achievments and what still requires maintenance before Winter's on-set.

There are many bright and beautiful flowers associated with August, Marigolds known for their golden hues symbolise warmth and are used for protection and positive energy rituals: Dahlias embody inner strength and creativity. Incorporate colours of orange, yellow and gold into your home to represent the warming sun and invite opulence and ampleness. Carve symbols of prosperity into candles before lighting them with intentions of affluence.

Crystals associated with August promote vibrancy and strength. August's birthstone, Peridot - known as the stone of compassion - is associated with rebirth. Citrine for success is perfect for carrying during harvest celebrations to invite positive energy. Amber, though not technically a crystal but a fossilised resin holds warm and nurturing energy. It's connected to the sun and is ideal for rituals centered around gratitude and grounding. Tiger's Eye offers protection and courage, which can be useful as you prepare for the coming Autumn.

The full moon within August is dubbed the *Sturgeon Moon*, named after the time of year when Sturgeon fish are caught from large bodies of waters and great lakes. This moon is all about perseverance.
This moon phase encourages introspection as the first signs of change in the season to advise us to be mindful of preparation and flexability.

By combining the abundant energy of August, you can create celebrations that are both festive and heartwarming. This approach blends ritual with comfort, ensuring that you can fully appreciate the harvest season while staying connected to the natural world and the joy of simple moments.

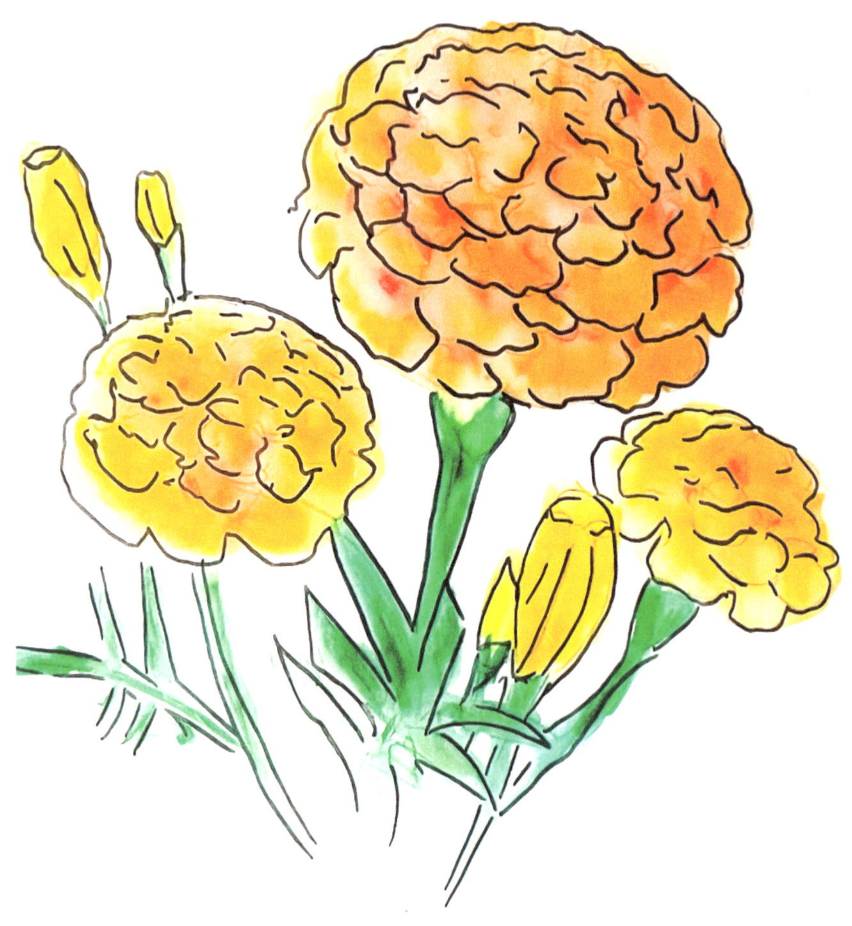

Herb - Laden Lullaby

Rosemary and thyme hang low,
By windows kissed with the moons soft glow,
An old book cracked, its pages worn,
Teaches me where spells are born.

I hum a tune, my voice so light,
As I prepare a spell of night,
Clove and cinnamon, sugars touch,
Add a warmth, not found in much,

A house that listens, beams that creak,
Walls that know I'm strong yet meek,
They hold my whispers, every sigh,
As star-clad clouds drift further by,

Peace is woven, stitch by stich,
This is the gift of a hygge witch,
A life of love in simple art,
Where every spell begins with heart.

Fire Element Motivation Spell

Purpose: Boost motivation and drive.

Ingredients: Red candle, cinnamon stick and tiger's eye stone.

Instructions: Light the red candle and hold the tiger's eye in your dominant hand. Rub the cinnamon stick between your palms to activate its energy.

Say, *"I ignite my passion and fuel my ambition." Carry the stone with you for motivation"*

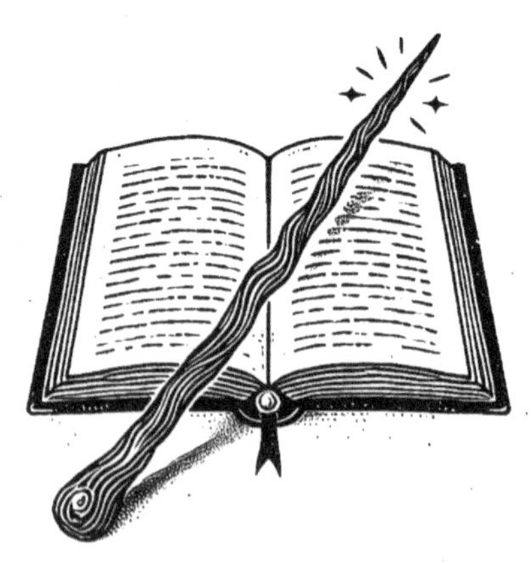

9

September

In September fields, the berries gleam,
A harvest rich, a summer dream,
We fill our baskets, hands stained red,
With Autumn's sweetness softly spread.

Back at home, the jars await,
We simmer fruit through evenings late,
The scent of jam fills every room,
Preserving Summer's fading bloom.

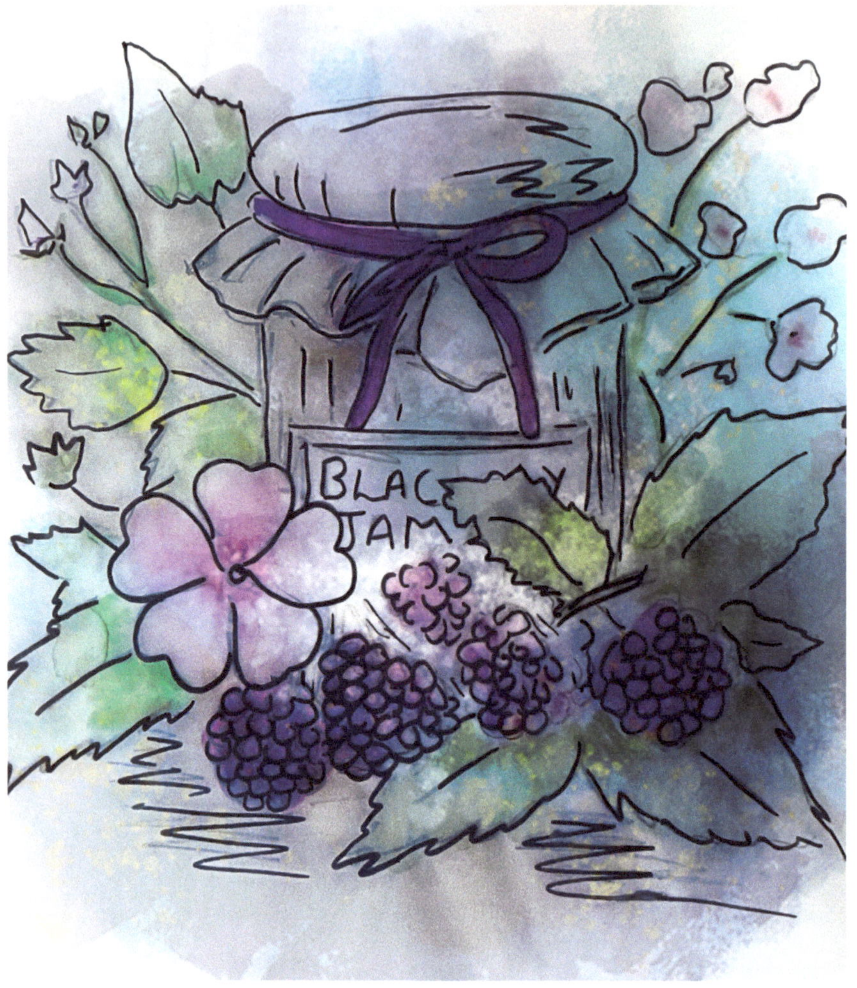

This is the time when we observe the equinox (between the 21st to the 23rd) during this phase there is perfect balance between day and night. We begin to usher in the change of the seasons and welcome Autumn. This is time to give thanks for the harvest and reflect on the fruits of labour and prepare for the coming Winter.

It is time to decorate your house with autumnal items like apples, pumpkins, acorns and colourful leaves.

September is traditionally when apple harvesting can start. These fruits are associated with knowledge and are often featured in many rituals giving thanks for their bounty. Apples can be used to bake apple pies or crumbles or make cider and juices.

Around the world, Apple Day is celebrated; this often falls somewhere between September and October. Apples have been employed for centuries for eating and drinking. On average it takes four to five years for an apple tree to produce its first reward.

Flowers associated with September are Chrysanthemums, which emphasise positive energy and security.

The Full Moon in September is known as The Full *Harvest Moon,* this moon transpires closest to the Autumn Equinox. Historically this moon provides additional light, which allowed farmers to work later into the evening to gather crops.

As the days grow shorter and cooler, September is an ideal time for baking and cooking hearty meals and taking part in mindful activities. This month is a time for balance, gratitude and preparation as the light and dark blend into harmony and the earth offers up its final gift before the cold ensues.

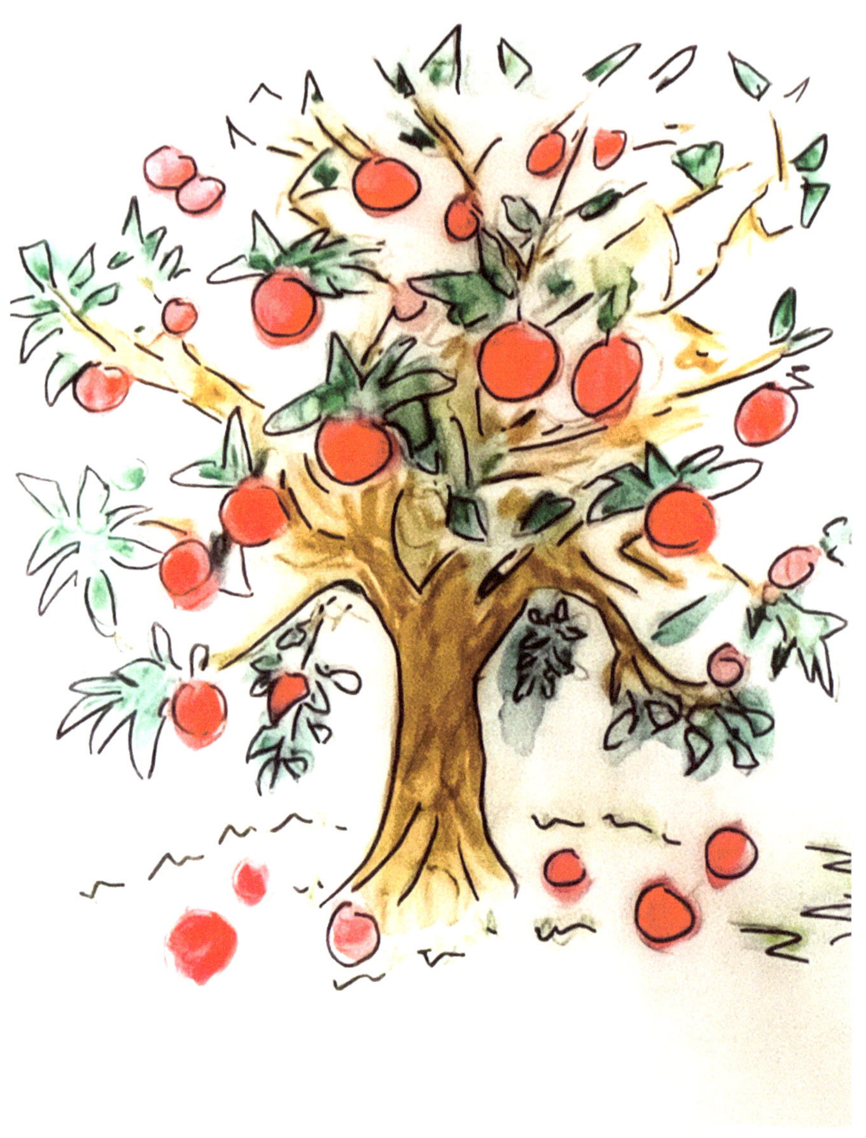

Autumn Equinox

Date: Around September 21st.

Significance: The Autumnal equinox is an bi-annual event when day and night are in balance. It marks the second harvest and a time to reflect on what we have reaped throughout the year, both in crops and personal acheivements.

Themes: Balance and gratitude, a moment of equal light and darkness symbolising stability within life. Harvest and preparation the last gathering of crops before winter. Reflection - as time to recognise and appreciate the abundance in one's life.

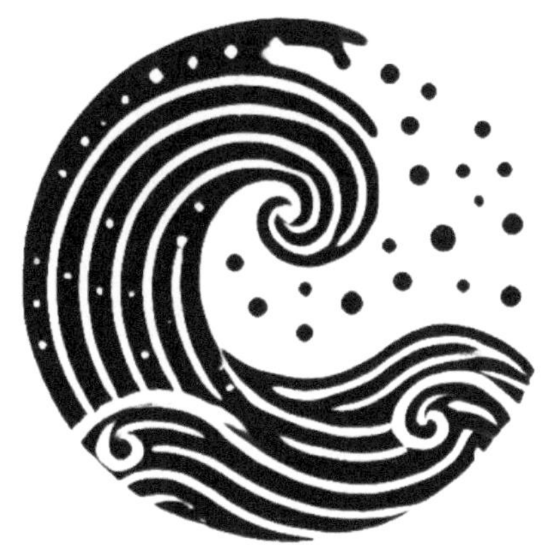

The Enchanted Window

A window seat, a quilt well worn,
Where morning yawns and poems are born,
The light glows soft, a golden brush,
Touching plants that crowd and hush,

Their leaves rustle, small and bright,
In secret talk with morning light,
I lean against the frosted glass,
Watching time in its gentle pass,

My cup is warm, my pages filled,
With notes of dreams and wishes willed.
Through scribbled entries, my thoughts take flight,
Guiding me through day and night,

This nook, a space of sacred pause,
Where magick plays without applause,
A place where echoes of laughter hum,
Inviting peace to always come.

Gratitude Spell

Purpose: Foster gratitude and mindfulness.

Ingredients: A small journal, Autumn leaves and a cup of warm tea.

Instructions: Write down three things you're greatful for each day. Place Autumn leaves as bookmarks to symbolise the abundance of the season. Drink the tea mindfully while reflecting on your gratitude.

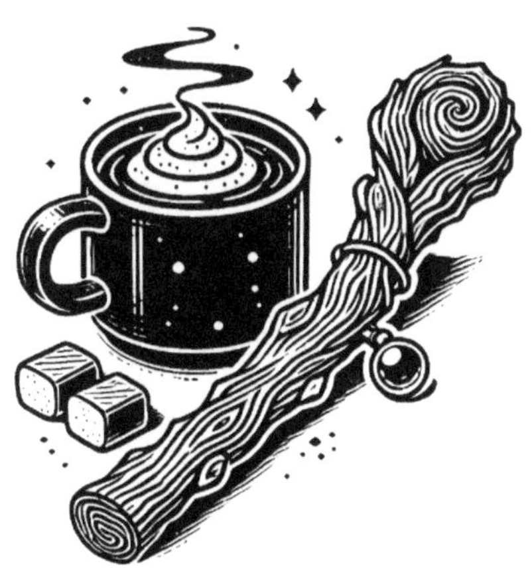

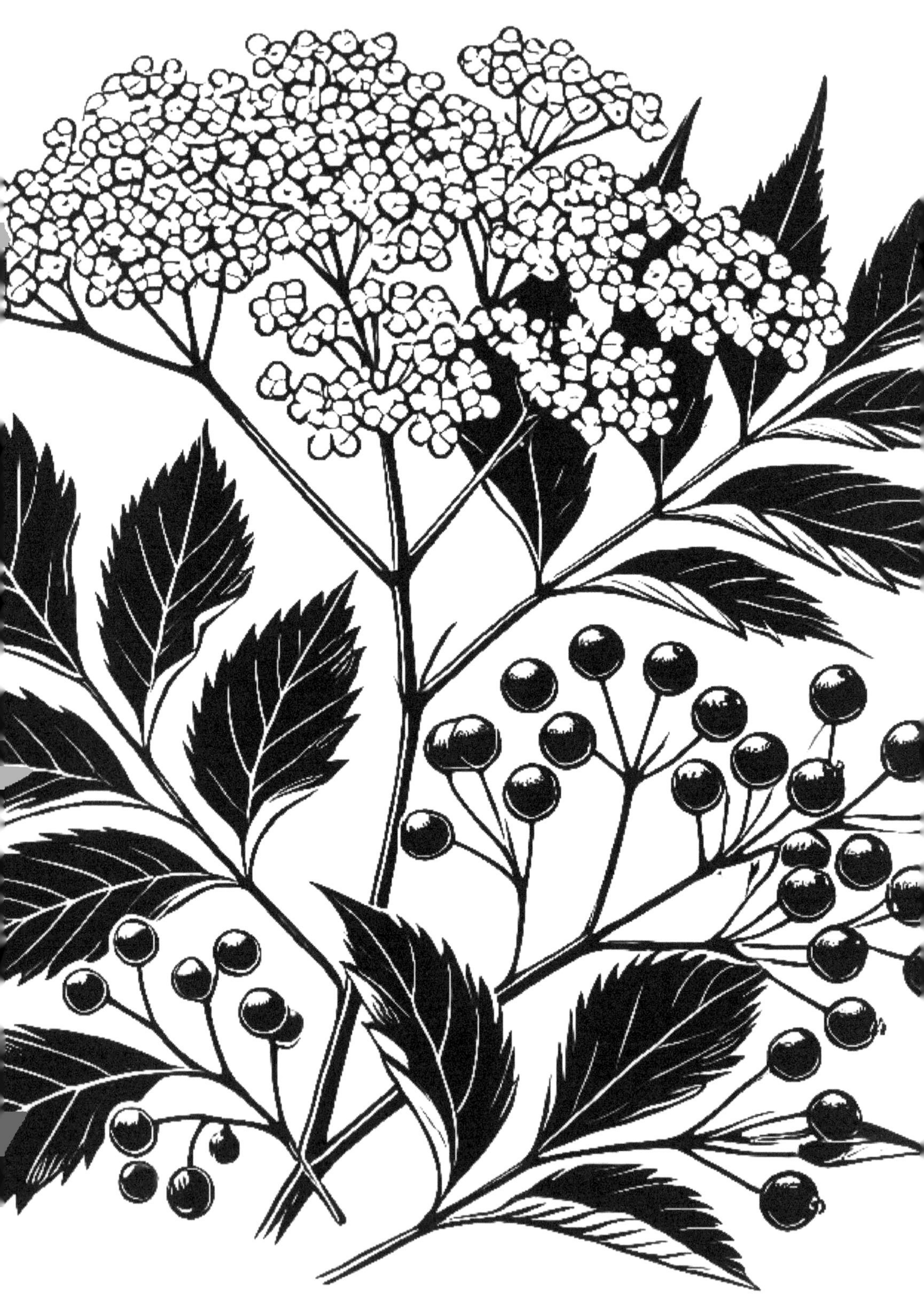

10

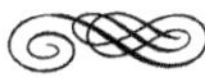

October

October whispers in cooling air,
Jack O' Lanterns, their warm glow fair,
Scents of cinnamon, nutmeg, clove,
Wraps us in this Autumn's alcove,

The nights grow darker, shadows stretch long,
Whistling winds hum an eerie song,
Leaves crunch beneath as the moon takes flight,
October's magick fills the night.

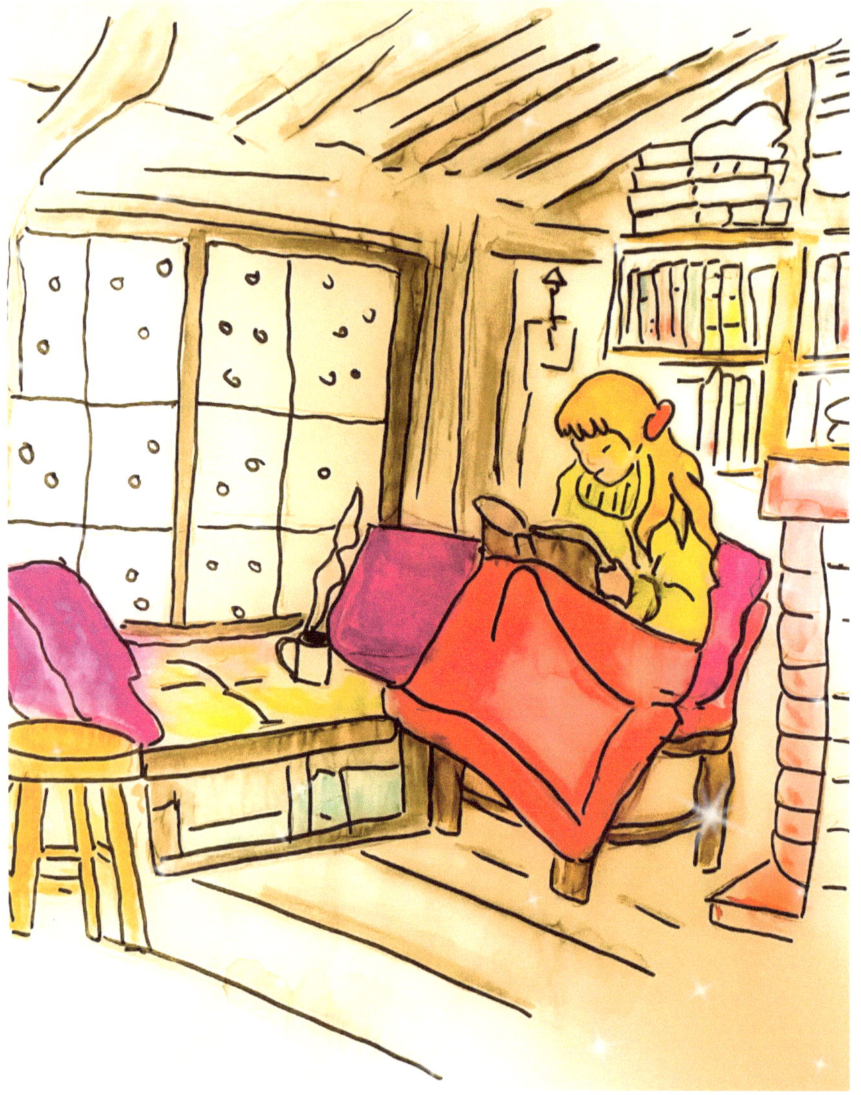

October has a certain significance, in that it heralds the end of the harvest and the beginning of the dark half of the year. This period is rich in practices which honour ancestry, the cycle of death and rebirth and the thinning of the veil between physical and spiritual worlds.

Some people attest that this is the best time of year for Shadow work as it can be effective for inner reflection and addressing ones fears, traumas or sub-conscious patterns. This is due to the alignment of the darker months and helps you to prepare for Spring.

Flowers which are asscociated with October include Calendula, whose bright autunmal colours can be used for protection; Black Dahlias which, surrounded by an ambience of mystery and aspects of power, symbolise and embrace the unknown.

The full moon in October is known as the *Hunter's Moon,* as traditionally they would look at the long Winter ahead and ensure food supplies were ample for the colder months - the bright moonlight was essential for a successful night's hunt.

The potent energy from the Hunter's Moon supports rituals that seek guidance from spirit animals and other spiritual allies.

Focusing on the cosiness of October, we can utilise these values with warm lights as the days grow ever shorter. Using extra blankets and throws, in fabrics such as wool or flannel in the requisite colours, or partaking in simple pleasures such as drinking warm beverages during our work ensures happiness and leads to contentment and well-being.

October is steeped in mystery, magick and preparation for many cultures and beliefs honouring the shift from light into darkness. The Hunter's Moon providing opportunity for reflection, spiritual preparation and connection to deeper cycles of life.

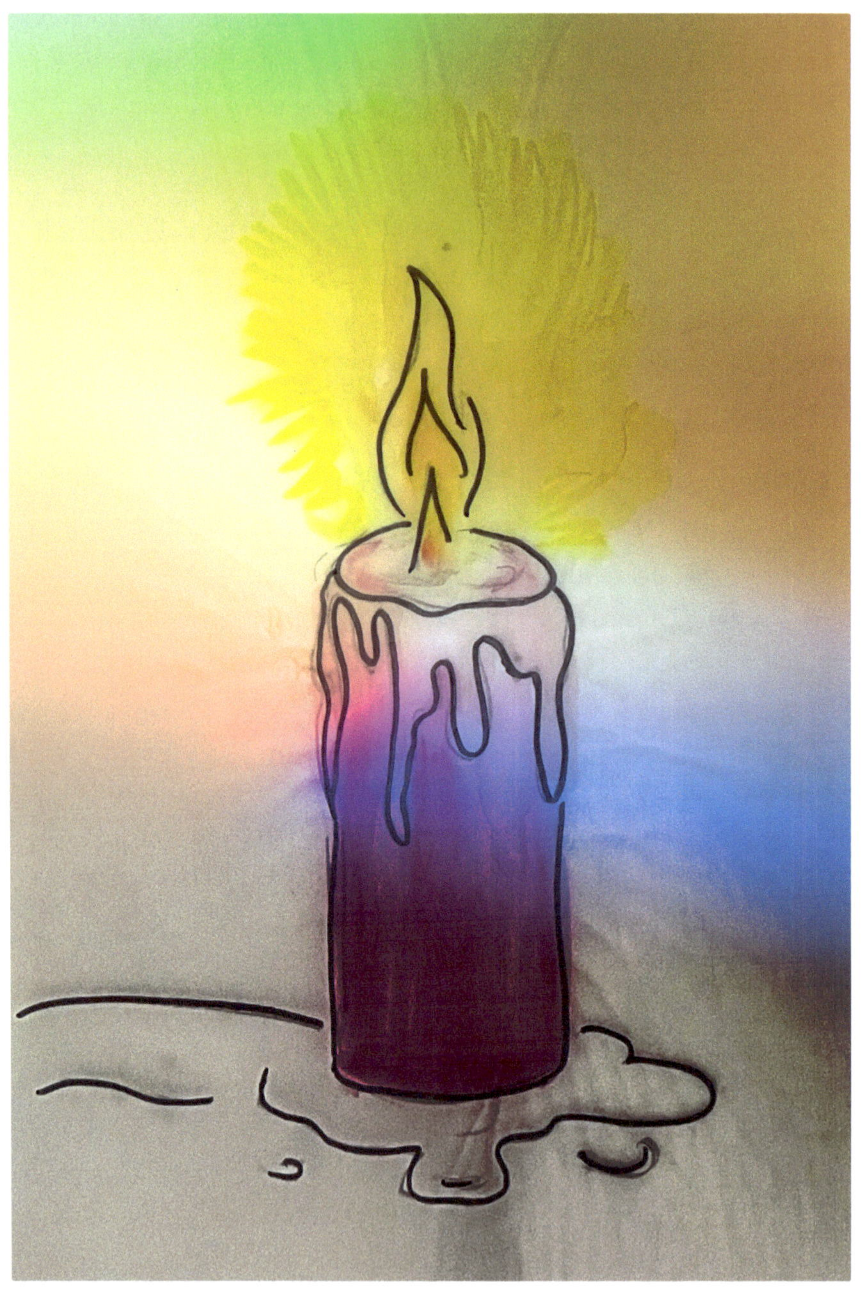

Midnight's Brew

A simmering pot, a midnight's brew,
Steam unfurls, as wishes do,
Chamomile, rose, a hint of sage,
Magick blossoms on this stage.

I write my words with careful hands,
A script a heart yet understands,
Every swirl of my wooden spoon,
Echoes under the watchful moon,

Candles melt, their scent unfolds,
As the story of the night unfolds,
Each flicker, a gentle jest,
Telling tales of warmth and rest,

I sip my brew, let it flow,
Through body and mind, calm and slow,
It's here I dwell, in this cocoon,
A hygge witch beneath the moon.

Ancestral Connection Spell

Purpose: Honour and connect with ancestors.

Ingredients: Black candle, photos of ancestors and mugwort incense or fragance.

Instructions: Light the candle and incense. Place photos in your sacred space and spend time speaking to your ancestors, inviting their guidance and wisdom. Let the scent of mugwort open your intuition.

11

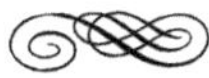

November

November's chill meets the oven's warm sigh,
Apple pies bake as sweet spices rise high,
In a loving home, the fire's gentle glow,
Fills the air with comfort, steady and slow.

By candlelight we sit, drinks in hand,
Music drifts softly, like waves on the sand,
Joy and love in every quiet space,
November's warmth in this peaceful place.

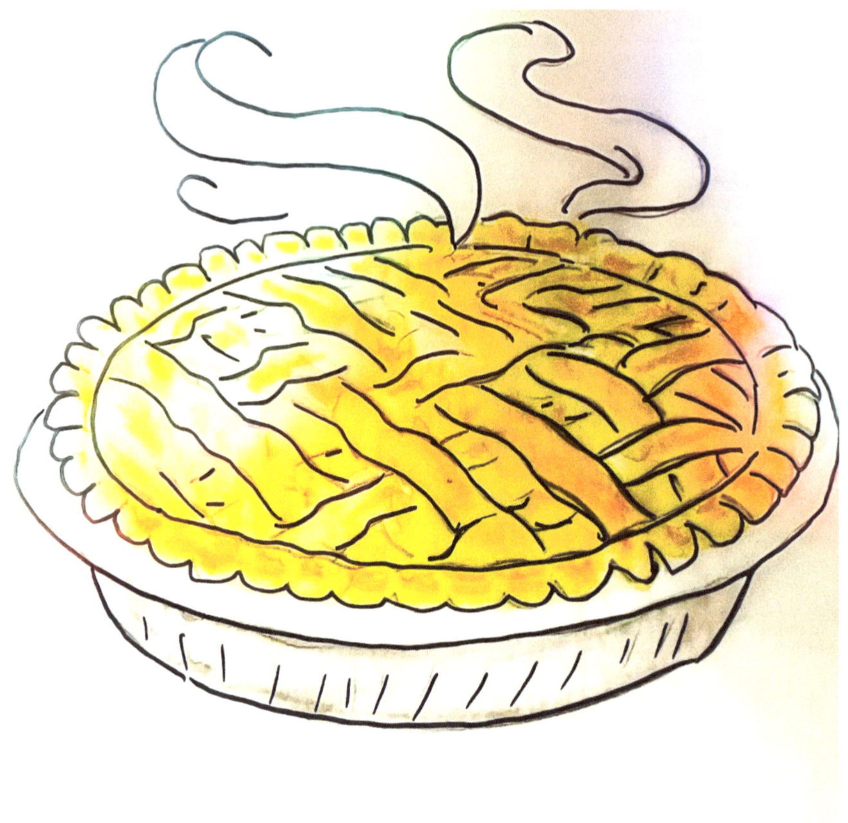

November is a quieter month, nurturing inner growth whilst we shift into the darker days and longer nights. The practice of cooking hearty meals should be in full force using nourishing foods, infusing them with love and gratitude. As Winter approaches, it's an apposite time to create protective spells and charms for the home using herbs for protection and to welcome the energies of the coming season. As the days grow colder constructing fires and lighting candles symbolise warmth and harmony.

Hygge practices can be seaminglessly woven into November's pagan themes of reflection, warmth and preparation. Burning essential oils and creating herbal baths with chamomile, rosemary and lavender after a long day allows us to stay connected to the natural world.

November is a time for stillness, gratitude and introspection. The *Beaver Moon* highlights the need to prepare for Winter, both physically and spiritually. Mores centered around ancestral connection and remembrance help maintain a sense of continuity and respect for the cycles of life.

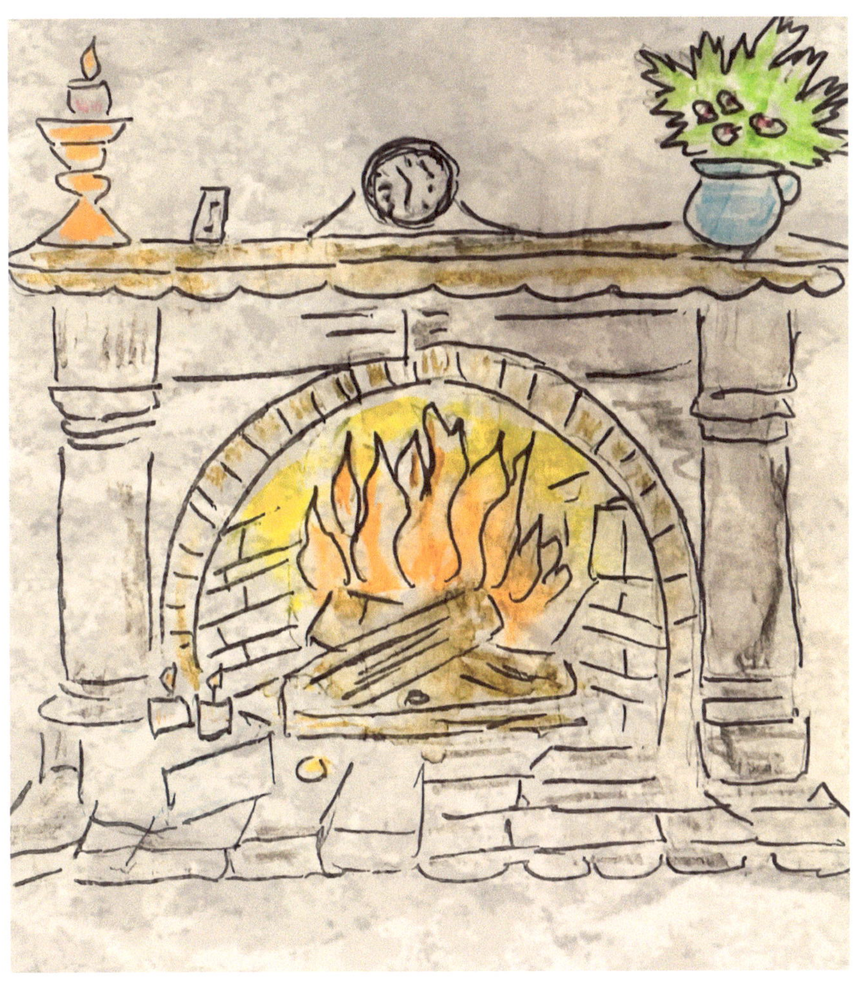

Fireplace Chants

A chant begins in whispers low,
As embers stir and cinders glow,
The fires heart, a pulsing red,
Listens close to what is said,

Bless this home, keep it strong,
Let love dwell where we belong,
Words of power in a voice so light,
Folded into flames delight,

A broom rests near, tied with twine,
Sweeping spells both fine and mine,
No rush, no race, just a gentle hand,
Guiding peace like grains of sand,

In this room, life's edges fade,
Each worry quelled, each ghost allayed,
A hygge witches warm domain,
Is magicks truest, sweet refrain.

Hearth Protection Spell

Purpose: Protect the home.

Ingredients: Bay leaves, cloves and a bowl of warm water.

Instructions: Steep bay leaves and cloves in the warm water. Use this infused water to sprinkle around the entrance of your home while saying,

"Guard this place, protect my space!"

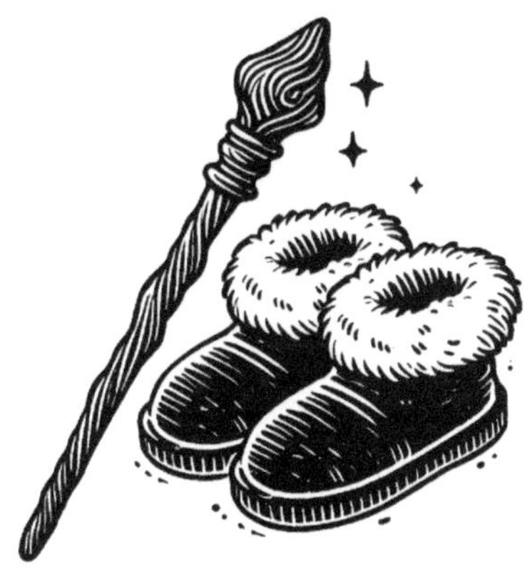

12

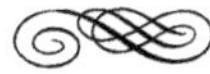

December

December's snow falls softly outside,
The sweet scent of pine fills the room inside,
An open fire warms our chilled feet,
While Winter's quiet feels gentle and sweet,

It's a season to rest, to slow and renew,
In stillness, we find a peace that's true,
Wrapped in warmth, as the cold winds blow,
We gather strength from the world in snow.

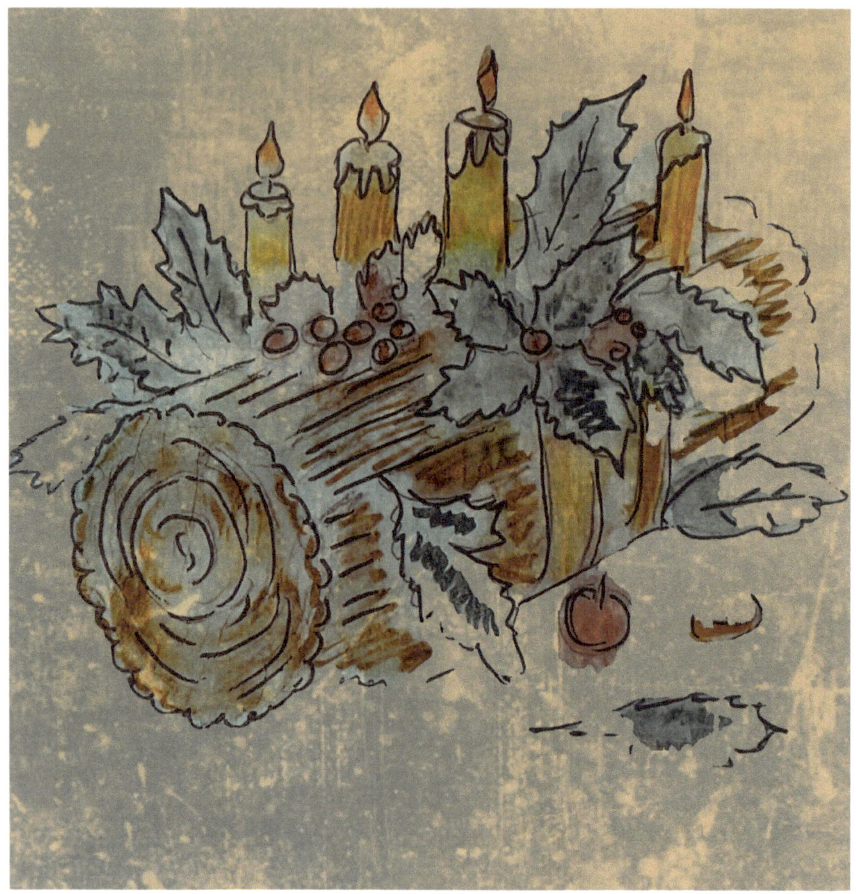

December is steeped in celebrations around the world as it marks the Winter Solstice and the rejuvenation of the Sun as the days gradually lengthen and symbolise renewal and the triumph of light over darkness. Yule is traditionally celebrated and has deep roots in Norse, Celtic and Germanic traditions; it was marked with feasts, fires and rituals to praise gods such as Odin, the Holly King and other Solar deities.

Key rituals during December include the Yule Log, Wassailing and decorating your home with evergreens, lighting candles and forging alter decorations in yellow and gold to represent the sun, alongside the use of items such as pine - cones, mistletoe, dried fruit and cinnamon sticks.

Holly and Poinsettia are flowers associated with December. Holly, renowned for its effervescence, red berries and glossy leaves, is closely associated with Yule and symbolises protection and resillience. It is said to ward off negative spirits and bring good fortune, hence its use in creating wreaths at this time of year.

Poinsettia, though more commonly connected to Christmas, symbolise the rebirth of the sun due to their bright red colour that represents the passion and vitality of the season as a whole. Mistletoe is another important plant; its sanctity, originating with Druidic traditions ensures that it is seen as a symbol of life. It is used in rituals for protection and love and is often found in homes as a method to invite blessings.

Evergreens are seen with Yule and Christmas. Pines, firs and cedar are fundamental as they represent eternal life within many cultures and traditions.

The Full Moon in December is known as the *Cold Moon* as it first occurs as Winter begins in the Northern Hemisphere. This time is a period for personal reflection, preparing for the New Year ahead and a good time to embark upon crafting projects such as knitting or making small herbal sacks to place around the house or to give as gifts.

December's celebrations are a harmonious blend of honouring the natural cycles, paying tribute to ancient traditions, and welcoming the return of light.

And the cycle begins anew...

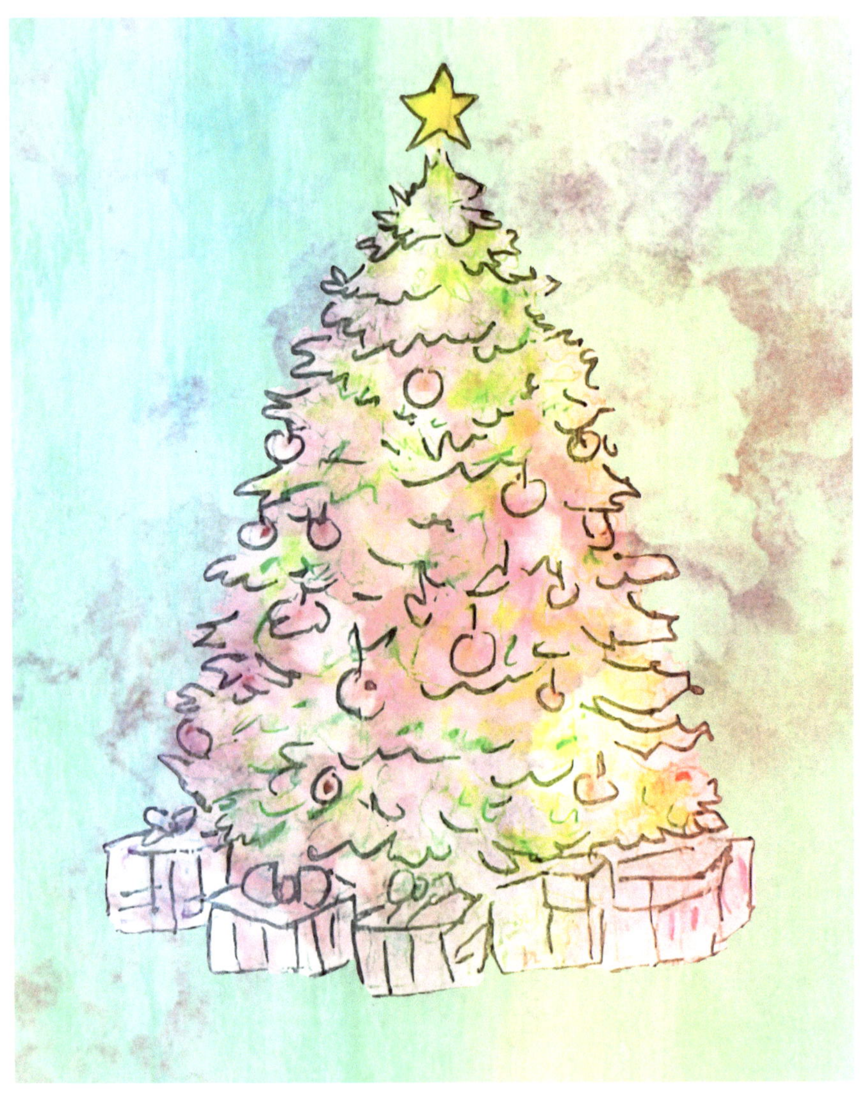

Winter Solstice

Date: Around 21st December.

Significance: The Winter Solstice is the shortest day and the longest night of the year, marking the rebirth of the sun. Yule is a time to celebrate the return of light and the hope it brings. It is a deeply reflective time that acknowledges the darkness but celebrates the renewal that follows.

Themes: Renewal and rebirth. The sun's return symbolises hope, renewal and the promise of brighter days. A time to reflect and look inwards, to connect with loved ones and embrace peace. It's a celebration recognising that light is beginning to return, even in the darkest times.

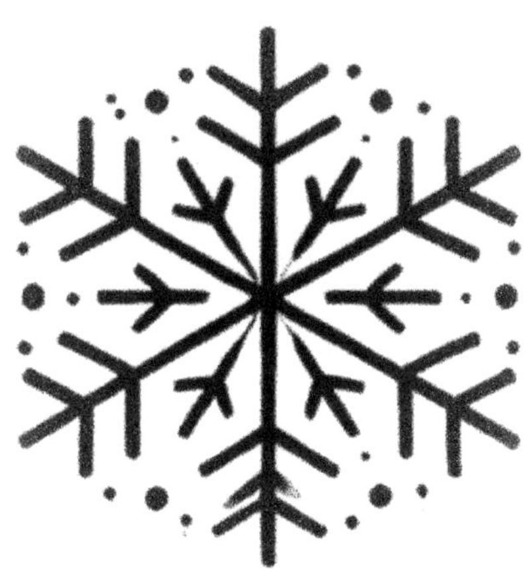

Spell Of Rest

Beneath the rafters, dark and old,
Lies a world in stories told,
I breathe the scent of baked delights,
Holding close these sacred nights,

My herbs are tied in bunches small,
Hanging there to a candle's call,
Lavender and mint, sage and lime,
Each a note in my grand design,

A charm for rest, an incantation,
Whispered in quiet dedication,
The house sighs, content and sure,
Within its walls, the spells are pure,

Magick isn't thunders cry,
It's the gentle hush as shadows lie,
It's the creak of floors, the sigh of rain,
A witches solace, free from pain.

Yule Candle Blessing

Purpose: Celebrate the return of light.

Ingredients: Evergreen sprig, gold or white candle and cinnnamon powder or stick grounded within a mortar and pestle.

Instructions: Decorate your altar with evergreen. Light the candle and sprinkle cinnamon around it, welcoming in the light's return.

Say, "As the sun is reborn, may warmth and joy fill this home."

Allow the candle to burn as long as is safe.

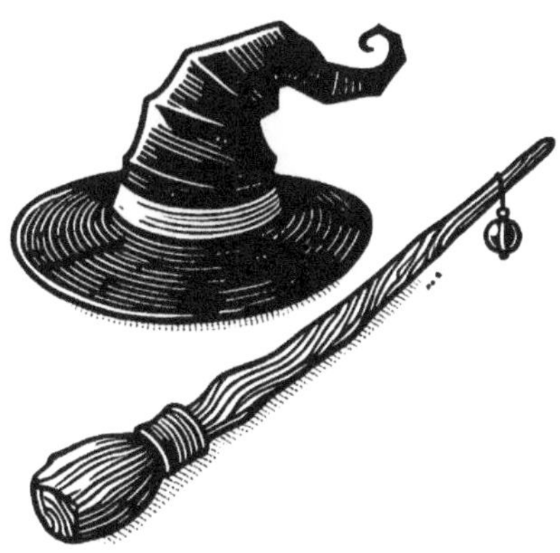

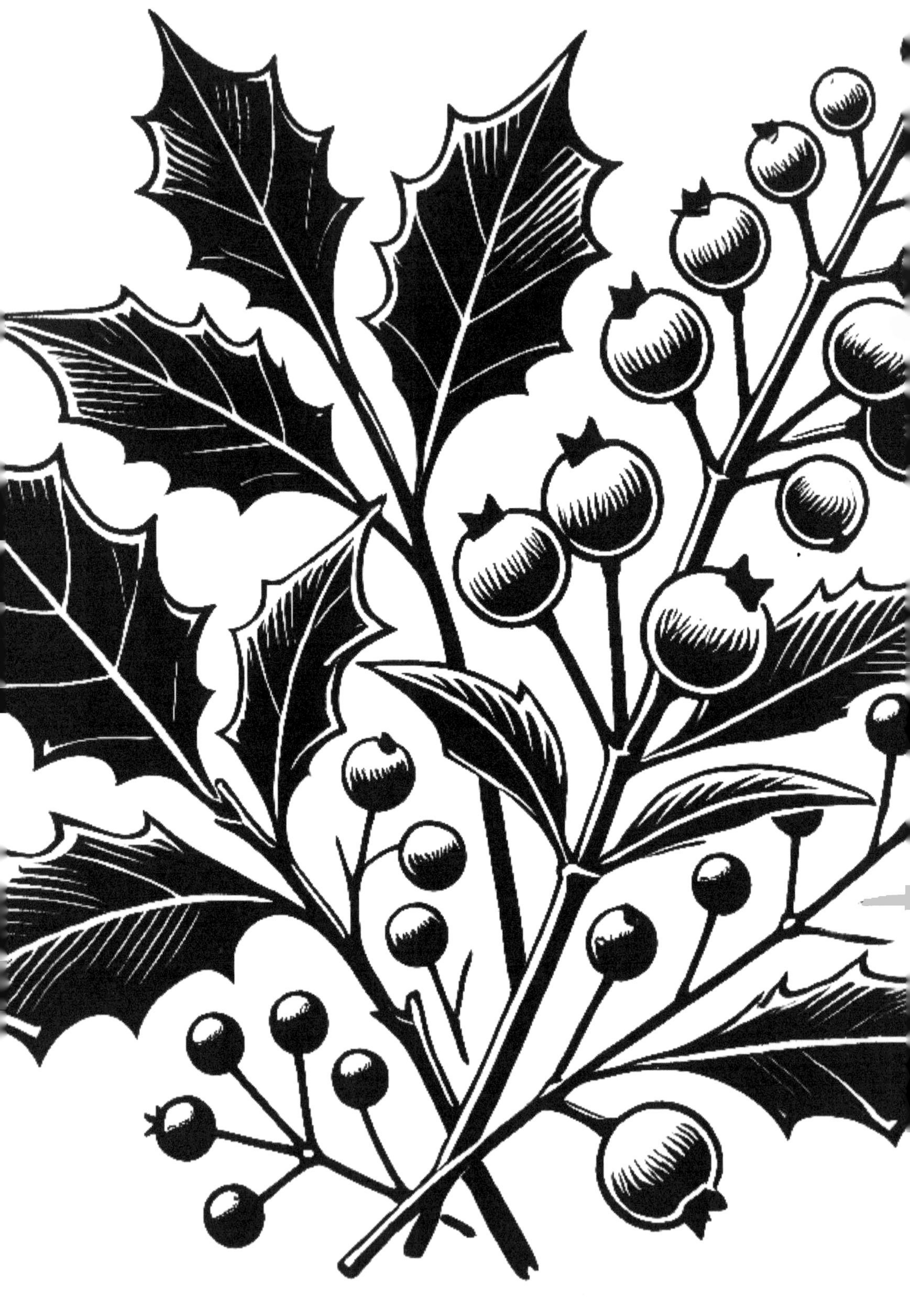

In Memory Of Snowy…

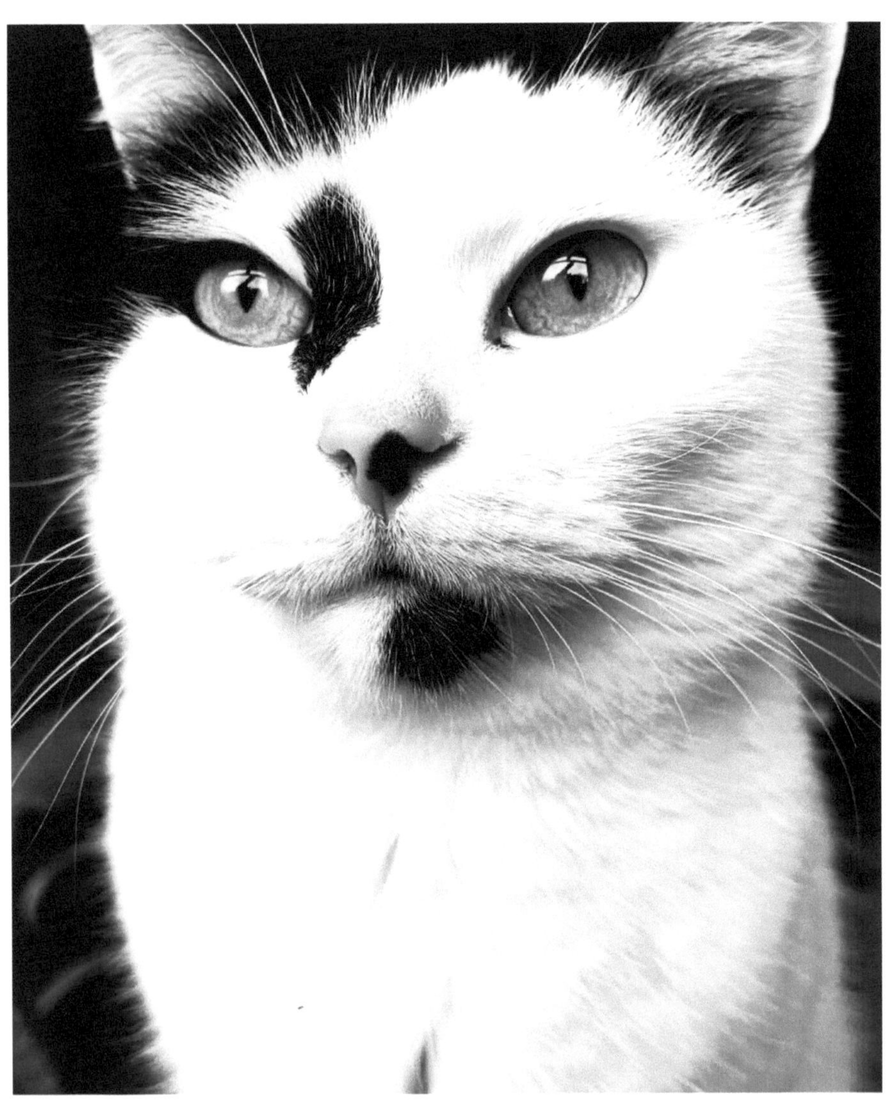

Snowy, with your soft coat of white,
A playful spirit, a spark of light,
Feisty and fierce, yet sweet as a dream,
A vibrant thread in life's fragile seam,

Oh, how you ruled, our small, gentle queen,
Keeping boyish mischief calm and serene.
Your tiny paws held sway, strong and true,
The ruler of hearts, adored by the crew,

The neighbours knew you, a friend to all,
You'd visit their homes, answer their call,
With a daring charm and a loving gaze,
You filled their days with your vibrant ways,

Five short years, but a lifetime of joy,
A firey girl with a heart to employ,
Far too soon you left our side,
And in our hearts, a void resides,

Yet in the breeze, we feel your purr,
A whisper soft. a fleeting stir,
Snowy, sweet one, though you're not here,
Your love remains, ever bright and near.

2019 - 2024

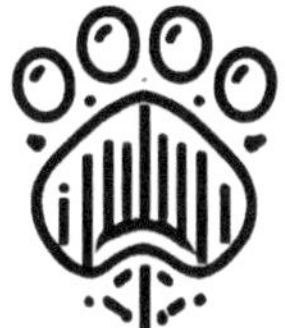

Author Biography

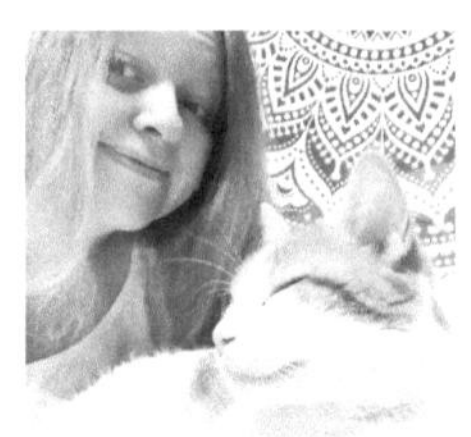

Charlotte Mann enjoys creating things and is based in Manchester, UK, where she lives with her partner, her two sons and their beloved cats. Her work is inspired by the beauty of nature and the joy of cosy moments, offering an escape from the hustle of modern life, through her poetry and art, Charlotte weaves worlds of comfort, reflection, celebrating the small wonders that ground us in a busy world. When she's not creating, you'll often find her amongst nature, drawing inspiration from changing seasons and for this book, the warmth of home.

Other Titles By Author

Nettle Nook - A Year In The Life Of An Allotment - May 2022

The Hygee Witches Almanac - December 2024

The Hedge Witches Almanac - March 2025

The Celtic Witches Almanac - June 2025

The Solitary Witches Almanac - September 2025